Praise for *Stop Complainers and Energy Drainers*

"Linda Swindling knows negotiation and how to stop work drama. As a leader you have to see the value in others and see through the excuses. You can't afford to have chronic Complainers in your company. Make the time to read *Stop Complainers and Energy Drainers*."

—David Irons
Senior Vice President, Sales/Marketing, Perfection Learning

"Nothing slows down a company's growth and innovation more than chronic Complainers. Linda Swindling's *Stop Complainers and Energy Drainers* gives you strategies that work to negotiate with those negative people and those time-consuming systems that just don't work. Buy the book. Follow the steps. Watch your business growth take off."

—Ford Saeks
Author of *Superpower: How to Think, Act, and Perform with Less Effort and Better Results*

"Toxic employees suck the life out of the companies they work for and the colleagues around them. The solution? Read Linda Swindling's *Stop Complainers and Energy Drainers*. This cheerful, fast-read book is practical, sensible and chock-full of no-nonsense advice that anyone faced with a Complainer can immediately put to use."

—Dick Grote
Author of *How to be Good at Performance Appraisals*

D0180922

"Linda Swindling shows you how to spot and stop every Complainer you'll ever encounter. You'll devour her data, you'll commiserate with her characters, and you'll celebrate her suggestions. Linda's practical strategies to address Complainers are easy to implement—even when the Complainer is you!"

—Elaine Biech
ebb associates inc;
Author of *Thriving Through Change*

"Ever felt the joy sucked out of a room? It was probably caused by some energy vampire bringing his or her misery and negativity. Linda Swindling gives you practical strategies to *Stop Complainers and Energy Drainers*. Get rid of those Toxics and energy suckers and bring on the joy . . . *because joy is the new competitive advantage!*"

—Amanda Gore
CEO of the Joy Project;
Author of *Joy Is an Inside Job*

"In today's wired, 24/7 workplace, successful people create maximum results in minimum time. To dramatically improve productivity, you must eliminate time-sucking, whining, negativity, and drama in your workplace. In *Stop Complainers and Energy Drainers,* you'll learn innovative strategies to handle toxic employees and energy-sapping environments. To gain higher performance from your team and regain your personal sanity, I highly recommend you read Linda Swindling's latest work."

—Laura Stack
Best-selling author of *Leave the Office Earlier*
and *What to Do When There's Too Much to Do*

"*Stop Complainers and Energy Drainers* is a user's manual for how to get more done. I recommend the book to anyone responsible for managing a team, growing a client base and providing sustained success."

—Derrick Jones
Director, US Distribution Sales, FLIR Systems

"We all know how the power of negative people in the workplace can ruin team spirit and affect productivity. *Stop Complainers and Energy Drainers* is a great tool to change the conversation, refocusing on what's most positive and productive. It's a must for any organization."

—Scott Friedman
Author of *Celebrate! Lessons Learned
from the World's Most Admired Organizations*

"For over 30 years I've helped companies overcome barriers to top performance. Along the way I've learned that one, just one Complainer, Whiner, or Toxic drama queen can suck the positive energy and productivity out of an entire team of great people. Until now, I've never had truly effective strategies to deal with Complainers beyond firing them or trying to ignore them. In her great new book, Linda Swindling gives me options, strategies, and solutions to finally stop Complainers and rechannel that negative energy in a positive direction."

—Joe Calloway
Author of *Be the Best at What Matters Most*

"Insightful! You will find yourself wanting to apply Linda Swindling's strategies as you read through the material. This is an excellent read for any organizational team-building session because it focuses on redirecting negative energy and funneling it into a positive resource. *Stop Complainers and Energy Drainers* validates that Complainers are needed because they foster change."

—Marilyn Stewart
Manager, Supplier Diversity, Alcatel-Lucent

"Like most organizations, our organization's success rests on the people who represent it. Every impression is critical. *Stop Complainers and Energy Drainers* is a mandatory read if you can't risk the message Complainers send."

—Cheryl Richards
Senior Vice President, Chief Diversity & Inclusion Officer,
Dallas Convention and Visitors Bureau

"To win in today's competitive business environment, leaders and senior managers must be able to execute brilliantly in up *and* down markets. They need people who contribute substantively to the organization's mission, not people who attack or sabotage it. *Stop Complainers and Energy Drainers* is a great action guide to eliminate negative, unproductive forces in the workplace so that managers and their teams can maximize innovation and bottom line results."

—Susan Battley, PsyD, PhD
Leadership Psychologist;
Author of *Coached to Lead: How to Achieve
Extraordinary Results with an Executive Coach*

"With this book, leaders now have the tools to develop a more positive work environment for everyone. The results are huge: less stress, more productivity, more creativity, even better health. No one should have to put up with negative people, especially since it's so preventable. Linda Swindling equips us with the answers and tools we need."

—Sandi Smith Leyva
President, BrainWays Training and Development

"This fun-to-read book is filled with seriously practical and insightful tips and techniques that stop Complainers and Energy Drainers. Linda Swindling addresses one of the most difficult tasks leaders must master: how to give feedback in negative situations. Her approach is masterful. This is a must-read for every leader!"

—Lenora Billings-Harris
Author of *The Diversity Advantage:*
A Guide to Making Diversity Work;
International Diversity Strategist

"If you deal with difficult people, get this book! Linda Swindling shows specific, usable and simple steps you can take to stop bosses, employees, and peers from engaging in destructive behavior. She also shows what you can do to save yourself when you can't make a change in other people. Look at this book as an investment in your future career—and sanity!"

—Terry Brock
Author of *Moving from Thinking "No Way" to "Not Yet!"*;
Professional Speaker; Marketing Coach

"How refreshing. Linda Swindling's book has taken the subject of complaining to a whole new (positive) level that managers can use to their advantage."

—Joseph C. Sherren, HoF
Best-selling author of *iLead: Five Insights*
for Building Sustainable Organizations

"We all know them, but rarely know how to keep from getting sucked into their drama. Linda Swindling gives you practical solutions that help you identify, understand, and deal with Complainers and the negative energy they create. She also helps you identify some of your own potentially destructive behaviors that can keep you from living your best life. Get out your yellow highlighter pen—you're going to need it!"

—Sandi Galloway
Director, Southwest MC&IT Sales Development,
Canadian Tourism Commission

"When you are searching for an employee for your company, you want the right person, in the right time, who can bring value to the organization. Quick advice . . . don't hire Complainers if you can avoid it. If they are already employed, stop them as fast as you can with Linda Swindling's advice. I've witnessed her negotiate and stop even the toughest conflicts."

—Phil Resch, Captain USN (Ret)
Principal Sandhurst Group;
Former Chairman CEO Netweavers

"This is a must-read if you want to deal with a very costly issue and impact your organizational culture in a significant way. Linda Swindling is spot-on in her insights for dealing with negativity in the workplace."

—Sam Silverstein, CSP
Author of *No More Excuses*;
Past President of the National Speakers Association

"Linda is an expert on complaining. You should have known her when she was a teenager."

—Linda's mom and dad

HOW TO
NEGOTIATE
WORK DRAMA
TO GET
MORE DONE

STOP

COMPLAINERS AND ENERGY DRAINERS

LINDA BYARS SWINDLING, JD

WILEY

Published by John Wiley & Sons, Inc., Hoboken, New Jersey.
Published simultaneously in Canada.

For general information about our other products and services, please contact our Customer Care Department within the United States at (800) 762-2974, outside the United States at (317) 572-3993 or fax (317) 572-4002.

Wiley publishes in a variety of print and electronic formats and by print-on-demand. Some material included with standard print versions of this book may not be included in e-books or in print-on-demand. If this book refers to media such as a CD or DVD that is not included in the version you purchased, you may download this material at http://booksupport.wiley.com. For more information about Wiley products, visit www.wiley.com.

Library of Congress Cataloging-in-Publication Data:

Swindling, Linda Byars, 1965-
    Stop Complainers and Energy Drainers: How to Negotiate Work Drama to Get More Done / Linda Byars Swindling.
        p. cm.
    ISBN: 978-1-118-49296-3 (pbk); ISBN: 978-1-118-859012-6 (ebk);
    ISBN: 978-1-118-859038-6 (ebk); ISBN: 978-1-118-859027-0 (ebk)
        1. Problem employees. 2. Corporate culture. 3. Business communication.
4. Personnel management. I. Title.
HF5549.5.E42S95 2013
658.3'045—dc23

                                                                                    2012044354

Printed in the United States of America

10 9 8 7 6 5 4 3 2 1

This book is for all the influencers who have invested their time, energy, and resources with me to help develop their potential and the potential of their people. Thank you for your trust and your experiences and for allowing me to be a part of your professional journey and breakthroughs.
Journey On!

Contents

Complainers Are Expensive

Is your company losing money because of constant Complainers? *Definitely.*

In today's economy, organizations expect the same or better results with fewer people to deliver. With jobs being downsized, "right-sized," offshored, outsourced, and eliminated, the demand for more output and better results with

1

fewer people has increased the workload and increased the stress! Complainers have fewer places to hide, and hard-working coworkers are showing less tolerance for those who complain versus contribute.

At first glance, reading a book that complains about Complainers appears counterproductive and an additional drain of your time and energy. *Take another look.* This book is designed to help you spot the type of Complainer you have, understand some of the reasons behind the behavior, and gain practical solutions to address and resolve the situation.

In this book, you'll see how to increase your ability to negotiate through the drama so that you can get back to work . . . and you'll have a chance to decide if you might be a Complainer who is draining other people's energy. This material is supported by statistics, research, and expert opinion.

Throughout the book you'll find the results of a recent survey of 1,014 people who work in a wide variety of industries. The survey was conducted electronically over a four-month period and designed to collect data about an individual's past and present work experiences. People were given the option to take the survey anonymously. In addition to 3 questions regarding demographic information, 11 questions were a mix of open-ended, single-select and multiple-select multiple choice responses with an ability to provide optional comments. Respondents gave descriptions of Complainers and examples of drains on their energy as well as the amount of time spent handling complaints, examples of complaints, days of the week people complained, and successful solutions. Participants were asked if they had left a job due to Complainers, if they would take a promotion with a pay increase that involved working with a chronic Complainer, and under what circumstances they could be a Complainer.

Survey responses are presented throughout the book in the form of graphs, actual quotes, descriptions, suggestions, and experiences woven into scenarios. Respondents revealed several surprises about Complainers and how to stop them. Unless designated, the numbers and percentages you see in the book are taken from this survey. Full results are found at www.StopComplainers.com.

Ten Business Reasons to Stop Complainers

1. The cost
2. Negative effect and loss of good employees
3. Legal ramifications
4. Environmental infection
5. Signal of problem or mental illness
6. Your sanity
7. Business reputation
8. Complainers' potential
9. Counterproductive strategy
10. The right thing to do

Reason 1: The Cost

Seventy-eight percent of people report a loss of at least 3 to 6 hours each week because of Complainers. At a minimum, that translates into 150 to 300 hours, or almost 1 to 2 months, spent *every year* for *every person* who spends time dealing with Complainers and draining situations rather than focusing on "real work" that produces results! Thirty-one percent say they spend more than 6 hours per week, and 2 percent report *more than 20 hours* of their time consumed during their workweek.

* How much of your time do Complainers, Interruptions, and/or Energy Drainers occupy in a week

Answer	0%	100%	Number of Responses	Response Ratio
0 to 2 hours			221	21.9%
3 to 6 hours			458	45.4%
7 to 10 hours			208	20.6%
11 to 15 hours			62	6.1%
16 to 20 hours			30	2.9%
More than 20 hours			22	2.1%
No responses			6	<1%
		Totals	1007	100%

This unproductive time costs companies at least $4,320 to $12,330 per year per employee. In a company with 100 employees, the figure equates to a weekly waste between $6,653 and $18,988 and a yearly waste of $332,640 to $949,410. That means that United States employers are spending at least a total of $10.1 *billion* on wasted time per week and over $505 *billion* a year on Complainers and draining situations.[1] These numbers do not take into consideration retention, retraining, productivity, and knowledge management or the unquantifiable number of customers, clients, and employees that Complainers drive away from your business.

Stop Complainers and Energy Drainers

To determine how much Complainers and Energy Drains could cost your organization in time wasted, go to www.Stop Complainers.com and use the Complainer Cost Calculator.

Reason 2: Negative Effect and Loss of Good Employees

Employees don't want to work with Complainers, even if you pay them. Seventy-three percent of people say they would choose to stay in their current job at their current annual pay rather than accepting a $10,000 pay raise if it requires working daily with a chronic Complainer.

If you don't address the work drama, you risk the loss of productive contributors. Complainers cause good employees to leave a company and jobs they like. At least 11 percent *left* a job because they couldn't stand working with a Complainer. This means culture rates above salary as a key component in why people, especially good performers, stay in their jobs.

Reason 3: Legal Ramifications

Employers have a legal duty to provide a safe workplace that is free from illegal discrimination; they must also comply with federal, state, and local laws. Complainers can create an illegal harassment situation in the workplace. Disregarding complaints about Complainers puts a company at risk for judgments, liens, and legal fees totaling thousands of dollars. Expect to pay between $50,000 to $250,000 in legal fees and potential settlements for each legal claim an employee brings in court against the employer, according to Mimi Moore, a partner in the labor and employment section of Bryan Cave, LLP.[2]

To further confuse matters, an employer might not be able to terminate an employee for *complaining* about their work conditions including posting on social media sites like Facebook or YouTube. If Complainers gripe about their work conditions or employment conditions and the company disciplines them, the Complainers may have a suit under the National Labor Relations Act.[3] Where Complainers are concerned, seeking employment advice *before* you act is less draining on your energy and your financials.

Reason 4: Environmental Infection

Work environments are a delicate ecosystem, and chronic Complainers infect their peers with their negativity and pessimism. Psychologist, author, and expert on organizational behavior Dr. Mel Whitehurst says, "Workers suffering from mild to moderate depression and anxiety infect other workers with anxiety and depression, spreading throughout the organization like a communicable disease. Entire work groups and even whole organizations can be contaminated with depression and anxiety." Companies can't afford further employee disengagement. In fact, a September 2012 Gallup poll reports that 52 percent of employees are not engaged and 18 percent are actively disengaged.[4] How many more employees do you need to hire to make up the difference for the lack of productivity?

Reason 5: Signal of Problem or Mental Illness

Complaining may be a sign of a major change to personal, family, financial, or health status. It can also signal alcohol, drug, and substance abuse or mental illness. Dr. Whitehurst says, "Researchers rank depression and anxiety among the three top workplace problems for employers." People who are depressed and anxious are more prone to complaining. However, persistent complaining, unstable moods, and erratic behavior are signs of a more serious mental illness.

According to the National Institute of Mental Health,[5] about one in four adults suffers from a diagnosable mental disorder in a given year, and about 6 percent suffer from a serious mental illness. Many times, managers and peers are among the first to notice a change in behavior. Addressing the complaining behavior alerts an employee to a potential problem. These conversations can influence employees to seek help in the form of coaching, counseling, and/or treatment so that they can function to the best of their ability on the job.

Reason 6: Your Sanity

Complainers wear on you and your mental well-being. Their drama can become your drama. In a sense, Complainers are crossing over into your lane of traffic instead of driving in their own. Instead of dealing with their own problems or moods, Complainers want others to feel their pain, notice them, address their difficulties, or even complete their work. Working alongside a chronically negative Complainer brings you down, disrupts your life, and isn't good for your health.

Doing others' jobs or coping with their issues is exhausting. There is a fine line between being a sensitive colleague who encourages good performance and one who attempts to fix every bit of drama in others' lives.

"Many leaders feel guilty or overly responsible, and say 'yes' when they or their resources are overextended," says best-selling author and psychologist Dr. John Townsend. "When leaders accept responsibilities that aren't theirs, they inhibit autonomy and responsibility from their direct reports, and do not help them grow. Clear boundaries help this process."

Reason 7: Business Reputation

Complainers can drive away your business. Customers talk. If they experience good customer service, they'll tell an average of 15 people. For bad customer service, plan on 24 others learning about it. These numbers increase dramatically if you have social media users. According to the 2012 American Express Global Customer Service Barometer, social media users "talk more." Give them a good customer experience, and they will tell an average of 42 people. Give them a bad customer experience, and they will let an average of 53 people know.[6]

Reason 8: Complainers' Potential

Yep, you read it right. If you manage them correctly, you can help channel some of your Complainers into more productive activities. Once Complainers learn better ways to communicate, handle stress, and be assertive, some of them may choose to transform into contributors.

Executive coach-consultant Elaine Morris says, "Complaining is a symptom of helplessness, low power, and a victim-like mind-set. Giving direct feedback and redirecting Complainers can allow them to see their own attitude is the problem. If they choose, Complainers can work on building their emotional intelligence, in particular, self-awareness, confidence, assertiveness, and problem solving. The potential to grow depends on their own willingness, and many people take that leap."

Reason 9: Counterproductive Strategy

Constant complaining does not work. Complaining without offering solutions creates a negative environment and takes the focus off solving problems. A benefit of having Complainers communicate better and bring solutions is the wealth of ideas and innovation your company can tap into. If Complainers choose to stop whining, criticizing, and creating work drama, their passion and energy can be redirected to problem solving and contributing to positive change.

A seasoned journalist with more than 25 years of experience, Lorri Allen says, "Reporters encounter a lot of mad, angry people who have complaints. But the people we take seriously are those who can channel frustrations into a positive solution and transform anger into a passion to effect change."

Reason 10: The Right Thing to Do

Leaders have an obligation to address behavior that isn't working. Your job as a leader is to give clear instructions, offer the proper tools, provide a safe workplace, define desired outcomes, monitor performance, provide feedback, and enforce company policies and standards. When you lead effectively, you remove one reason high performers leave. By holding people accountable for their work and professional behavior, you encourage people to solve the problems they can. Often, Complainers will either elect to perform up to standards or will self-select themselves out of the organization by quitting.

In more than 20 years of negotiating employment situations as an attorney and a mediator, then later as a business consultant, one truth is clear: people want to contribute to the success of their organizations. To achieve results, they want to feel personally empowered to solve their own problems and enjoy their work environment. Leaders want to encourage employees to do their best work and experience personal growth.

More than anything, people and the people who lead them want the drama at work to STOP.

Introduction:
How to Use This Book
with No Complaints

Negotiate Your Way to Success

Complainers are energy drainers who create messy, inconvenient work drama. The disruptions they cause involve negative emotions, illogical behavior, irritants, and interruptions to getting your job done. Here are travel tips to help you negotiate your journey through this book with no complaints.

> How do you know if you have a constant Complainer? People are happier to see him or her *leave* for a vacation than *return* from one.

This book is all about spotting problems and fixing them quickly. It helps you *spot* how your Complainer is causing work drama so that you can *stop* the behavior and get back to work. Complainers are found at all levels and in all industries.

Occupations of Survey Participants

* Please check the professional field that best applies to your occupation:

Answer	0%	100%	Number of Responses	Response Ratio
Attorney/Legal			22	2.1%
Accounting/Financial/Banking			78	7.6%
Sales/Marketing/Public Relations			133	13.1%
Education/Academia			96	9.4%
Manufacturing/Construction/Logistics			31	3.0%
IT/Technical			66	6.5%
Engineering/Science			54	5.3%
CEO/Business Owner/Entrepreneur			63	6.2%
Healthcare/Medical			32	5.1%
Insurance/Underwriting/Financial Services			34	3.3%
Nonprofit/Professional Association			48	4.7%
Meetings/Hospitality/Restaurant			50	4.9%
Organization Development/Training Speaking			26	2.5%
Property Management/Real Estate			17	1.6%
Retail			12	1.1%
Counselling/Psychology/Social Services			12	1.1%
Human Resources/Staffing			42	4.1%
Military/Government			19	1.8%
Travel/Aviation			9	<1%
Clerical/Administrative			49	4.8%
Other (View all)			92	9.0%
No Responses			9	<1%
		Totals	1014	100%

Whether the Complainer is your boss, a peer, or one of your employees, you'll find examples, explanations of the behavior, conversation strategies, and suggestions to stop the Complainer from generating additional problems. You'll see negotiating suggestions for all stages of work drama including approaching your leadership for support. The term *negotiating* is used intentionally throughout this book. Negotiating is a strategic and much stronger approach to stop work drama than managing, dealing with, or handling.

It's no revelation that complaining is a common occurrence at workplaces. Like others, your top Complainers are probably coworkers and team members, employees who report to you, clients or customers, your boss or people you report to you, family members, or close friends.

Who Complains or Bugs You During the Workday?

* Who complains or bugs you the most during the workday? Please select your top 3 only. ◆ ◆

Answer	0%	100%	Number of Responses	Response Ratio
Coworkers or team members			678	67.8%
Employees who report to you			284	28.4%
Your boss or people you report to			224	22.4%
Suppliers/Vendors			112	11.2%
Clients/Customers			268	26.8%
Business partners/ Contractors			91	9.1%
Family members or close friends			221	22.1%
Spouse or girlfriend/ boyfriend			118	11.7%
Other (View all)			62	6.2%
		Totals	1000	100%

Note: Other included telemarketers, students, volunteers, citizens, and union members.

13

Complaint Department

It's true. Benefits do result from *constructive* complaining. However, if you're reading this book, it is more likely that you are experiencing venting, whining, or griping that isn't effective but is downright annoying. Chronic Complainers are self-absorbed. Their complaints aren't helpful. They create a hyper-focus on negative issues. Complainers aren't concerned with solutions or correcting a dangerous situation. They are focused on themselves. These self-focused agendas generate stress, tension, and depression both in the workplace and at home. Chronic Complainers suck the resources, time, energy,

Complainers Complain About These Things

* What types of things are they complaining about? Please select your top 3 only.

Answer	0%	100%	Number of Responses	Response Ratio
Job fear and/or pressure to perform			174	17.4%
Unclear direction or lack of feedback from leadership			303	30.3%
Too much work to do			362	36.1%
Deadlines			148	14.7%
Reorganization or change in work environment			185	18.5%
New boss			23	2.3%
Unrealistic demands from clients or customers			223	22.3%
Incompetent vendors, suppliers or contractors			86	8.6%
Incompetent coworkers or boss			273	27.3%
Inadequate pay or benefits			101	10.1%
Health issues			47	4.7%
Personal or family issues			223	22.3%
Not feeling heard or respected at work			173	17.2%
Just feels good to vent or let off steam			199	19.9%
Being micromanaged			96	9.6%
Disagreements with coworkers			160	16.0%
Other (View all)			76	7.6%
		Totals	1000	100%

Note: Other included current affairs, politics, economy, taxes, location of work assignments, budget cuts, lack of clients, technology issues, and sports teams.

and joy out of work and life. Their top complaints are: too much work to do; unclear direction or lack of feedback from leadership; and incompetent coworkers or boss.

Complainers use whining, complaining, or offensive behavior to gain rewards and/or to avoid some type of pain. For many, their bad behavior has worked since childhood. In fact, chronic Complainers are often compared to school bullies, spoiled toddlers, whiny children, sneaky adolescents, and sullen teenagers. Complainers are called many names.

Which of These Complainers Sounds Familiar?

Rachel is a Whiner who works in her company's benefits department. This morning, she sighed and started griping to her boss Bill. "I'm tired of all these changes. No one asks for our opinion when they 'improve' the technology around here. They don't ask if we need the upgrades, if we want them, or if they will help us. . . . Well, these changes aren't

(continued)

Introduction: How to Use This Book with No Complaints

(*continued*)

helping me. I'm not going to use them. In fact, I'm just waiting for someone from the IT department to ask me for information about their benefits. I'm going to be just as helpful."

Bill, her manager, shook his head. He thought, "Of course Rachel wouldn't take the time to understand the latest upgrades to the system. She didn't learn the last ones. Rachel wastes far more time and energy griping than it would take her to learn the upgrades." To avoid hearing her whining, Bill reformats Rachel's work every day. He decides that doing the extra work is easier than listening to her constantly moaning and groaning. *Chapter 1 explains what Bill can do to negotiate with a Whiner employee like Rachel.*

■ ■ ■

Tim is Brandon's lead on the marketing launch and a Controller. Tim is a bully and demanding. Brandon spent the past two days with no sleep, ensuring the research and visuals were ready for Tim's presentation tomorrow. Brandon went to bed an hour ago and was finally getting some rest. At 12:30 AM his phone rang. It was Tim on a speakerphone. "Hi, Brandon. It's Tim. I was worried about you. You're not answering your cell. We're up here working past midnight on this major launch, and you're at home sleeping. I guess we know who wants this launch to occur and who lets their teammates work through the night with no help. Well, sweet dreams." Brandon lay frozen for 15 minutes thinking through Tim's critical remarks and his options. Should he wait until the morning for Tim to cool off or call him back now? Could he stay alert enough to drive back to the office? Should he start looking for another job? *Chapter 4 explains what Brandon can do to negotiate with a Controller boss like Tim.*

■ ■ ■

Evelyn is Heidi's peer and a Toxic. Most of Evelyn's peers believe she is pure evil and avoid doing any work with her. The sales vice president likes results and believes Evelyn produces them. In reality, Evelyn doesn't produce anything on her own but conflict. Evelyn is smart. She makes it difficult for others to protest about her because she complains about others' performance and work ethic first. And Evelyn is unpredictable. You never know which Evelyn will show up at work: the one who makes you feel special and takes you under her wing, or the one who is vindictive and stabs you in the back. Other employees who crossed Evelyn are no longer with the company. Today, Evelyn took credit for her peer Heidi's work. Evelyn hadn't originated the business or even helped move the client case forward. Evelyn has complained in the past about Heidi's performance and work effort. Heidi is drained, depressed, and sick of Evelyn's manipulation, but Heidi desperately needs the job. *Chapter 5 explains what Heidi can do to negotiate with a Toxic peer like Evelyn.*

Decide on a Direction

You have a choice in how to use this book to your benefit. For example, you can decide to go directly to the chapter that addresses your Complainer's specific behavior to stop it.

Different types of Complainers use complaints very differently. You might be surprised what you uncover. You can look at your Complainer's reactions, learn the reasons for his or her behavior, and decide the best strategy to negotiate a solution.

There are other ways to use this book to prevent complaining. If you experience work drama from several sources—or if your Complainer has several complaining traits—you may want to read from the beginning to the end. Later, keep this book as a reference manual or a road map for handling future work drama. (Disclaimer: *Nothing* herein remotely suggests that one of the ways to use this book is to throw it at a Complainer. Despite your frustration, bodily harm is *not* an acceptable strategy.)

To maximize your success, please take the free online assessment "Spot Your Complainer's Type" at www.Stop Complainers.com. Then, read through the rest of the Introduction to understand the signs you will need to successfully negotiate work drama.

Types of Complainers

First, spot your Complainer's type with the assessment. One of the surprises of the research was identifying more than one kind of Complainer. In fact, survey respondents identified *five* types of Complainers. Each type of complaining has its own communication style, including tone, word choice, and accompanying behavior. The five types are seeking different outcomes, from empathy and attention to stability and control. This book gives you specific communication strategies to refocus each Complainer type.

You can identify the types of Complainers by taking the free online assessment to "Spot Your Complainer's Type." Then, determine which of the five categories of chronic Complainers you're facing:

- **Whiners** complain by showing disapproval, venting, or withdrawing (Chapter 1).

- **Complicators** employ complaining tactics that frustrate, complicate, and create confusion (Chapter 2).

- **Prima Donnas** complain by seeking attention, gossiping, creating drama, and stirring up trouble (Chapter 3).

- **Controllers** use a variety of aggressive complaints in their attempts to reach an outcome, to control situations, and to control people (Chapter 4).

- **Toxics** are dangerous individuals who use complaints and misinformation to manipulate and poison the environment to further their self-absorbed agendas (Chapter 5).

Road Signs to Help You Negotiate Success

Here are signs you will find throughout the book to help you successfully negotiate your way:

 These quotes and descriptions of Complainers and energy draining situations were provided by survey respondents.

These common **R**eactions help you spot each type and provide ideas of the **R**eality or the reasoning behind that behavior. Identifying some Complainers can be tricky. If all of the behaviors don't match or if they adopt traits from other types, be prepared to attempt different strategies until you find solutions that work.

 These are actions that don't work to address your Complainers or Energy Drains.

 This suggests turning to management or human resources (HR) to ask for help.

 These strategies show you how to turn the situation around and successfully negotiate work drama.

 These travel tips help direct you as you move forward to get more work done.

Communication Strategies

Spotting the type of Complainer you have is the first step. Communicating in a way that stops the negative behavior is the next. People negotiate with their Complainers in several ways:

 Letting them vent

 Listening and trying to solve their problems

 Redirecting their focus or changing the subject

Stop Complainers and Energy Drainers

⚠ Keeping conversations professional

⚠ Avoiding them and screening phone calls

⚠ Ignoring them or leaving

⚠ Agreeing and joining in the complaining

⚠ Asking them to stop

⚠ Reporting them to leadership or writing them up

Other survey responses included:

⚠ Getting angry

⚠ Telling them life isn't fair

⚠ Having no idea. Coaching; mentoring; nothing seems to work

> To increase the likelihood your Complainer hears suggestions for improvement, approach conversations with objective feedback mixed with a genuine desire for him or her to succeed.

In the chapters that follow, you'll find words to use in negotiating with your Complainer. See what works and what doesn't. In Vistage, a worldwide development organization for chief executive officers (CEOs) and key decision makers, the members and leaders use the term *carefrontation*. Carefrontation means "I'm confronting you regarding your behavior or actions in a caring manner." Or "I care enough about you to give you my observations." Several "rehabilitated"

Complainers said that it took a carefrontation type of conversation to open their eyes that their behavior wasn't working.

Most chronic Complainers *won't* stop complaining without a lot of effort on their part. However, once you understand what kind of Complainer you have, you can develop a strategy to get that Complainer to stop complaining to you!

If You Are the Complainer

It is amazing how many people admit to being a Complainer or a reformed one. If you think you may be a Complainer, take the assessment "Are You Seen as a Complainer?" at www .StopComplainers.com. After you receive the results from your assessment, read more in Chapter 6 to determine which complaining behavior resembles your own. You'll read about examples of Complainers, good reasons to stop complaining, and effective communication strategies that work to get you what you want.

Research shows that people can become Complainers when faced with Energy Drains. Energy Drains are those environmental factors, organizational constructs, and systems and processes that cause you unnecessary stress. In Chapter 7 you can determine the Energy Drains that are causing you or your people stress. Negotiate the Energy Drains successfully, and that negative complaining behavior and unnecessary drama at work and at home can stop.

Complaining isn't always a bad thing. Chapter 8 of this book shows you ways to create logical arguments, negotiate work drama, gain support, and be heard by decision makers. You'll learn how to stop *constant* complaints without blocking *constructive* ones, to value information that comes with complaints, and to complain effectively when it's necessary. These last chapters are dedicated to helping you obtain helpful feedback and improve your odds as you negotiate work drama.

So, You Want More

You have *plenty* of tools to help you implement what you've learned. In the Resources section, you'll find two "Complain-a-Grams" that you can copy and send anonymously to either your Complainer or a company leader. There is a "Conversation Strategies per Type" table where Complainers are linked to familiar communication styles, such as CORE MAP, DiSC, Myers-Briggs, BrainStyles, and Personal Insight Inventory. This correlation helps you identify development opportunities that can improve coping skills and enhance a Complainer's natural strengths. You also have "Negotiating Work Drama Checklists" to help you form your strategy and communicate your position effectively.

And please, go to www.StopComplainers.com. There you'll find additional resources including the assessments, a calculator to help you determine the cost of your Complainers, downloadable "Complain-a-Grams," checklists, interview questions, articles, and the full survey results. Okay. You have everything you need *and more*. It is time to start reading and *stop complaining!*

Chapter 1

Whiners

Help Me Across

⚡ Martyrs   ⚡ Pouters

⚡ Spoiled brats   ⚡ Soap opera actors

⚡ Dark clouds   ⚡ Weeds/exploders

Spot a Whiner

Whiners remind you of holding children's hands as you walk them across a street. They want you to help guide them through life's challenges. Whiners complain to connect with others. They seek reassurance, guidance, and direction. Whiners complain to reach out and get empathy or validation from others in their community. They need constancy, support, and security.

Are You Negotiating with a Whiner?

Whiners complain to form relationships and receive empathy. They vent, withdraw, and want others to solve their problems. Whiners:

- complain about how things aren't fair.
- play the victim and are powerless.
- always seem to have something wrong in their lives.
- are always upset about something or someone.
- never bring solutions, only problems.

Reactions. Whiners bring doom and gloom to the office. They are overly sensitive, withdrawn, moody, sulky, grumpy, and crabby. They are passive lamenters who pout, sigh, and moan. They repeat discussions regarding perceived offenses or slights. Whiners withdraw, hide, become quiet, and exhibit helplessness. If frustrated, they become touchy, explosive, and prone to outbursts and tantrums.

Reality. Whiners hope to be soothed, comforted, or reassured. They feel if they let others know their complaints, the issues will be addressed or solved for them. When they feel overwhelmed, ignored, or vulnerable, they explode.

Stop a Whiner

 Actions that Don't Work with Whiners:

- **Giving reasons their reaction is irrational or unproductive.** Whiners are not concerned with rational outcomes or the inconsistency of their actions. They want empathy, not logic.

- **Forcing them into problem solving before they vent.** Whiners have to release their emotions and feel heard before they are open to solutions or a proactive approach. Trying to make Whiners feel better by complimenting them won't help, nor will telling them to "grow up."

- **Venting along with them or solving their problem.** Whining with them just encourages more complaining. When you provide an opinion or offer solutions, they usually reject your advice or make excuses. On the rare occasion they accept and act on your suggestion, they will blame you if the result is bad. And, if the advice works, you now become their crutch for making their future decisions.

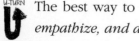 The best way to negotiate with Whiners is to *listen, empathize, and ask for solutions.*

- **Listen.** Whiners are trying to connect and build relationships through their complaining. Seems counterintuitive, doesn't it? Spending a few minutes actively listening and even mirroring back what you hear from Whiners goes a long way with these relational Complainers. Note a "few" is less than 5 minutes . . . you're not their counselor.

- **Empathize.** Simple sentences such as, "That has got to be tough," "Wow, I'm glad I don't have that problem," or "I don't know how you do it," are sufficient. Also, it may be all the empathy Whiners need. You may hear a Whiner respond, "It really isn't that bad," "Thanks for listening," or "Sorry. I just needed to vent."

- **Ask for solutions.** Ask Whiners for solutions and repeat as needed. Remember, chronic Whiners know that whining gets results. They may need several exposures to "Wow. What are you going to do about that?" before taking the hint that you aren't the best place to deposit their problems.

How to Stop a Whiner Boss

When the Whiner is your boss, you need to listen and make sure you aren't causing the problem and that the solution isn't yours to fix. Like all Whiners, bosses want to feel heard and receive empathy for their problems. Sometimes they would like someone else to fix the problem, and sometimes they just want to vent. Listening can make all the difference as long as you don't sign up as your Complainer's professional coach, counselor, or parent. Despite the role as your leader, you still need to *listen, empathize, and ask for solutions.*

Human Beings, not Beans

Zoe works as a case manager for a nonprofit social services agency. She sat down next to Cindy, her boss, and the executive director at their annual volunteer appreciation lunch. Zoe soon regretted not finding another seat. Cindy said hello and asked how Zoe was doing. Two seconds after Zoe replied, "Fine," Cindy started whining:

"That must be nice. I'm not fine. You work with people and get to solve problems. You're not stuck having to account to a board of directors for every penny. You don't have to explain why costs are up and our donations are down again this year. It's unbelievable. You know, we're here to serve people who need the help. If I wanted to be a bean counter, I wouldn't have chosen a career in social services."

 He reminds me of a whiney 2-year-old. (He's 52.)

U-TURN Zoe needs to *listen* for a few minutes. Cindy is venting. Reporting to the board is not a problem under Zoe's control. Then, Zoe should *empathize* with Cindy's situation. Finally, Zoe should *ask* Cindy what *solutions* she is going to try—and then *repeat* as needed.

Zoe's response might sound like this: "Wow. All that reporting can't be any fun, and it takes time away from your important work. What are you going to do?"

Let's say Cindy's response is, "Well, what can I do? I can't just make donors give us money or stop inflation. I can't avoid the board's questions. I can't ignore the finances. What can I do?!"

Zoe can repeat: "I'm sorry. Sounds like you want a change. What do you think you're going to do?"

How to Stop a Whiner Peer

When the Whiners are your peers, you often care about them and may see others doubting their skills because of their behavior. Remember, it's not your role to tell them it's time to get past a problem or attempt to lead them. Giving solutions on how to fix the drama won't work until Whiners decide to change. On some level, Whiners attract or encourage continuing conflict. Remember to *listen, empathize, and ask for solutions.*

Soap Opera Life

Julie is a sales professional at a large hotel. Julie's life story could fill a book, but people would probably think it was fiction. After two years of Julie being at the hotel, her coworkers Janet and Tahnesha have become experts in the details of Julie's soap opera. Julie's constant complaints of an abusive husband, a child who graduated college and refuses to visit, financial woes, health challenges, mother-in-law issues, and a chronically sick cat make working with Julie exhausting. Julie's sick and vacation days are a welcome break for the hotel's sales team. Julie's latest rant was:

"Did I tell you that he's getting angrier and meaner every day? I just can't leave him. Besides, where would I go? Not everyone takes pets. He'd let Snowball die just to spite me. She's the only one who loves me. If I leave, my monster-in-law would be thrilled. She'd have her precious son to herself. But what if Chloe comes to her senses and comes home? She's only 23."

He won't get help. He is a professional victim.

U-TURN The shared feeling among the hotel staff is that daughter Chloe is the smartest family member for leaving that nuthouse. Janet and Tahnesha need to *listen* to Julie for a few minutes. Then, *empathize* with Julie's situation. They need to remember that Julie needs professional emotional guidance, not well-intentioned advice from her coworkers. Janet and Tahnesha might want to notify their human resources (HR) professional who knows the hotel's health benefits. HR may be able to point Julie toward a good resource or an employee assistance program to assist her in sorting out her issues. Finally, they need to *ask* Julie what *solutions* she has to address her problems and *repeat* as needed.

After listening for a few minutes, Janet's or Tahnesha's response might sound like this: "Wow. Julie, I don't know how you do it. I couldn't handle all the problems you have. What are you going to do now?"

If Julie says, "I just don't know. It is so hard," the response is, "Sounds like it is really hard. So how are you going to handle it?" Repeat as needed. Eventually, Julie will understand that although caring and empathy exist, there are limits.

How to Stop a Whiner Employee

When the Whiners are your direct reports, they want to feel heard and reassured that their contributions are also important. They want their leader or a "person in power" to solve their problems. As their leader, your job is to point out areas where they contribute to the company's success and where their behavior or performance is not adding value. Remember to *listen, empathize, and ask for solutions.*

Financial Fred

Fred works for a large national distribution company. He inadvertently received an e-mail file from the compensation group. Before realizing what the e-mail contained, Fred opened the file and saw a spreadsheet containing the salaries of several of his coworkers. Since Fred found out his coworkers' pay is higher than his, he hasn't been the same. Despite a strict company policy to keep pay confidential, Fred gripes about the difference to his family members, friends, other employees, and even customers. Although he could go to company-sponsored courses to improve his skills, he has chosen not to attend.

> Reminds me of a child who found out that someone else got more candy, more dessert, or a bigger allowance.

 Fred's leader should *listen* for a few minutes. Then, *empathize* with Fred's situation. Finally, he should *ask Fred what solutions* he has to address the problems and *repeat* as needed. Fred was fine with his pay until he knew others made more.

During a conversation to discuss his pay, his boss could say, "I'm so sorry, Fred. What are you going to do about making more money?"

Fred's response might be along the lines of, "What do you mean, what can I do? You're the boss. You could give me a raise tomorrow if you wanted."

If so, his leader can reply, "Fred, you're at the highest pay grade for your job description. Because of your seniority, you have more vacation than anyone else. If you want to increase your value to the company, which would also increase your pay, you need to learn new things that the company needs. You haven't attended any of the company classes to learn anything new. What are you going to do?"

 ## Turn to Management to Help Stop Whiners

When turning to management to help with Whiners, remember to ask and answer several questions.

How Does the Company Benefit by Helping You Negotiate with a Whiner?

Whiners bring doom and gloom to the office. They aren't problem solvers; instead, they waste people's time with their tales of woe and expect others to solve their problems for them. They can be overly emotional and indecisive, and they may not act when they should. All of these are good business reasons for someone in management to help you negotiate with a Whiner.

What Do You Want the Organization to Do?

If you are a peer or a direct report, you may need help with guidance, strategy formulation, or intervention. As a leader, you want HR or a senior manager to support your decision to act. Whiners can cry, pout, and throw temper tantrums. You should consider having an HR representative as you coach or counsel the Whiner in case that person becomes emotional. If not, let management and HR know that you are about to have such a conversation. Your leaders need to know that your Whiner may come to them crying or upset. Some Whiners are known to leave for the day after speaking to their boss. You want your leaders to be prepared to support your position that the whining behavior stop.

What Communication Strategies Work with Whiners?

As you plan for discussions with Whiners, remember that they want others to empathize with them. They will gripe or emotionally withdraw to get their needs met. Whiners are introverted and feeling communicators. Under extreme stress, they "blow" and throw temper tantrums. As the leader, let your Whiners know that you appreciate and care about them personally. Suggest Whiners seek training or coaching to develop their natural strengths in conflict resolution and team building and to improve coping skills in assertiveness and communications. **Remind Whiners that people want to connect with them more when they are problem *solvers*, not just problem *suppliers*.**

What Detours and Roadblocks Do You Face?

Whiners know that complaining works in getting them what they want. At times, their "helpless me" act bonds them to more powerful people who can protect them. The same companies that have no problems disciplining people for excessive absenteeism, poor performance, or rule breaking may be hesitant to discipline a Whiner because it seems they already have it so rough.

 My Complainer reminds me of a beaver—always gnawing on something.

U-TURN Turn Management Around

The best way to negotiate to get help with your Whiner is to show that the Whiner's choice to play a victim is hurting others' performance and wasting time. Document a Whiner's specific behavior and language, especially when other teammates are affected by that person's inaction. Remember to be detailed as well as solution-oriented in your conversations with management and HR. If you paint a clear picture of the helpless act and how a Whiner is offloading work to others and hasn't made a contribution, other leaders in your company will take notice of the whining behavior, too.

Travel Tips to Stop Whiners

Here's what you need to know before you attempt to negotiate work drama with Whiners:

 Reactions. Whiners *appear* as martyrs, spoiled brats, dark clouds, and pouters. They are overly sensitive, withdrawn, moody, sulky, and crabby. If frustrated or extremely stressed, they become touchy, explosive, and prone to outbursts or tantrums. They are passive in their approach and lament, sigh, moan, act put upon, or discuss personal details of their life.

Reality. Whiners *want* you to hold their hand through life's challenges and fix their problems. Through their complaining, they are seeking reassurance, guidance, direction, and a connection to others.

 It doesn't work to solve Whiners' problems, offer advice, or tell them to grow up and act like an adult.

 The best way to negotiate with Whiners is to *listen, empathize, and ask for solutions*.

Listen. Give them your full attention and actively listen for a *few* short minutes.

(*continued*)

(continued)

Empathize. Let Whiners know you heard them and you care by saying things such as, "Wow, that has to be tough for you" or "I don't know how you do it."

Ask for Solutions (and Repeat). Ask for a problem-solving approach or a solution, such as, "How will you handle that?" or "I'm glad I don't have to deal with that. What are you going to do?" Repeat as much as needed.

Chapter 2

Complicators

Slow Uphill Climb

⚡ Critics	⚡ Diverters
⚡ Nitpickers	⚡ Historians
⚡ Know-it-alls	⚡ Micromanagers

Spot a Complicator

Negotiating with Complicators reminds you of slowing down to climb a steep upgrade. Complicators are impeding, obstructing, criticizing fault-finders who delay and hamper others. They complain to maintain their sense of stability and control. Complicators are passive-aggressive in their approach. They feel comfortable with a lot of information and details. To maintain their version of order, Complicators create systems, procedures, and processes that aren't easy to navigate. Complicators are masters of minutiae.

Are You Negotiating with a Complicator?

Complicators complain to avoid change and maintain stability. They frustrate, complicate, and create confusion. Complicators:

- delay and put up roadblocks if something new is offered.

- nitpick and criticize others' work.

- bring up past failures and mistakes.

- protect systems and information.

- use knowledge and details to confuse and complicate matters.

 Reactions. Complicators use specific terminology or complex rules that confuse those who deal with them. They are stubborn and use complaining to identify flaws in proposed plans, point out incompetence in others, block attempts at change, and conceal areas in which they feel incompetent.

Reality.   Complicators grow impatient and push for details and facts to make sure they are precise and accurate. Their complaining increases when they lack information or knowledge. They block actions or ideas that disrupt their need for certainty, order, logic, and stability. Complicators feel threatened if someone "invades their turf" by questioning or overseeing their organization or area of responsibility.

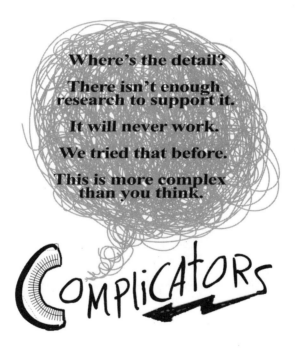

Stop a Complicator

Actions that Don't Work with Complicators:

- **Telling them to be team players.** Relationship appeals or directives aren't the best approach for people with logical sensibilities. Avoiding them or excluding them from team meetings will backfire. They complicate and criticize solutions created in their absence and become more protective of information and systems.

- **Trying to change their minds.** Complicators spend a significant amount of time preparing their position. They are stubborn and defensive when you attempt to change their stance or thinking.

- **Asking them to adopt a more positive attitude.** Encouraging Complicators to be more supportive of others and their ideas isn't a good strategy. Complicators are concerned more with being right and having correct systems than improving relationships and maintaining a positive image.

> He was a brick wall with a mouth . . . no ears to listen, no way through it.

 The best way to negotiate with Complicators is to *reduce speed, respect effort, and upgrade.*

- **Reduce speed.** Slow down. Complicators need time to reflect and notice the impending change. Leaving them out of conversations will slow you down later. With their skeptical style, prepare for questions, resistance, diversion, and debate. Be prepared to over-communicate with them and provide sufficient details and support.

- **Respect effort.** Complicators are afraid of change or not having adequate knowledge. Complicators fear someone will discover they don't know as much as they portray. Find a way to acknowledge the intellect that went into Complicators' systems, methods, thought processes, or designs. Complicators need to be correct and want to be appreciated for the accuracy of the specific tasks they complete.

- **Upgrade.** To reduce Complicators' defensiveness, present changes or new information as a logical addition, next step, or revision. Ask Complicators to help you fine-tune, implement, and integrate the "upgrade" to make it a seamless piece of their existing processes or plans. Seeing a change as an add-on or revision is less frightening than seeing it as something new.

How to Stop a Complicator Boss

When a Complicator is your boss, you need to identify the reasons behind the complaining behavior. Like all Complicators, bosses complain to protect their stability and control of a situation. They worry about not being accurate. They want data to be correct and want systems to operate seamlessly. A Complicator boss resembles a micromanager or perfectionist who criticizes and distrusts your abilities. Despite the role as your leader, you need to *reduce speed, respect effort, and upgrade.*

> ⚠ My Complainer refuses to change with the times. He is constantly trying to force everyone to think his way. He goes on and on, repeating the same old stuff over and over again. It never changes.

Boomerang Boss

It was the fifth time Ted had gone to Sheila to approve the client report. Sheila was in charge of interfacing with one of their most important clients. She is particular about her reports and feels like her presentation format is the best way to promote the engineering firm. At first, she asked Ted to add graphs. Then, she wanted bullet points instead of numbers. Sheila corrected her own revisions twice and changed her mind about the color of the graphs. Ted knows the client cares most about getting a quick answer before an opportunity is lost, and he knows the excessive revisions are delaying their response. As Ted went to make the next change, Sheila said:

"Ted, this is important and needs to be right. Your report is a reflection on me and this company. This client is one of our most important. Everything we send needs to be clean, clear, and concise."

As Ted left her office, he heard Sheila complaining on the phone, "Really, I don't know how Ted was ever hired. He has an easy assignment that he can't seem to get right."

> ⚠ This Complainer always critiques other people's work and looks for them to make mistakes.

 U-TURN Ted needs to *reduce speed*. Racing around and saying there is a deadline will not speed up Sheila. She is complicating *because* she knows this information is important to the client and she wants to get it right. Sheila may not think that Ted's information is accurate or that he has spent sufficient time on the report. Ted needs to *respect the effort* Sheila has put in and acknowledge that Sheila has built a strong relationship with the client. He needs to show Sheila his supporting data and ease her worry about the quality of his research and preparation. Ted needs to let Sheila know that getting the information to the client is an *upgrade* to the services they are delivering and the proper response at this time.

Ted's conversation might sound like this:

"Sheila, I spoke with the client earlier today. My contact stressed that we need to get the information to them as quickly as possible. I've done my research and shown you the detailed support. You've agreed with me that the recommendations are accurate. I know formatting is important and is one reason we've been able to maintain such a great relationship with our clients. On this occasion, the client has reassured me that it would be better to have the information now than wait until we have it perfect and lose the opportunity. Do you think we could send the report as it is now so that we can meet their deadline?"

How to Stop a Complicator Peer

When a colleague is a Complicator, his or her complaining behavior results in obstructing, nitpicking, and micromanaging and impeding progress. Complicators create confusion, invent illogical rules, or require compliance with complicated policies. They conceal information and impede the progress of the entire team. Complicators fear that change will keep them from maintaining their version of order. Complicators worry that others will find flaws, determine they are incompetent, or somehow take control of their organizational process. As a peer, your role is not to inform Complicators that their systems are outdated or to tell them to just "get over it." Instead, *reduce speed, respect effort, and upgrade.*

Queen Beatrice

Beatrice is the office manager at a large medical facility. She started 25 years ago when the practice was just beginning and established all the office processes. She is fond of telling the staff that she knows where all the skeletons are buried.

Ian was hired to transfer the charting and patient medical documentation into electronic format and to ensure the office meets current standards. Beatrice isn't providing Ian with essential information or access to get it. Apparently, Beatrice is griping to other staff members that Ian is too pushy and moving at lightning speed. Beatrice's bosses have no idea she is so uncooperative with Ian. When she and Ian meet with the doctors, Beatrice smiles and nods to show she knows about the importance of transferring the information. When she called today, she told Ian:

"I'm sorry. I have to cancel our meeting again. There's an office emergency. You're asking for a lot, so you'll have to be patient. I can barely manage everything on my plate. I can squeeze in about 5 minutes tomorrow. Maybe we can meet sometime next week to discuss what's already working and what you really need."

> ⚠ This person is allergic to learning something new.

 U-TURN Beatrice is the "queen bee" of the office. She hopes that if she complains and continues to block Ian's attempts to change long enough, he will go away and leave her systemized beehive alone. Ian needs to *reduce the speed* of the change. He should acknowledge Beatrice's system and *respect the effort* for the order she has created. Next, he needs to ask for her input and help as they *upgrade* the system. Ian could say:

"Beatrice, I appreciate the effort that went into creating your system. Most offices aren't as well organized and don't have this level of depth. As we upgrade, I want to make sure the specifications work best with the system in place. I can do it, but I would hate to attempt to implement the technology and risk messing up your organization without your help."

If Beatrice continues to block him, Ian can send the owners and Beatrice a status update via e-mail describing what he has accomplished to date. He could add that he and Beatrice are scheduled for their initial meeting tomorrow to ensure the updates meet her specifications and their deadline. This approach gives the owners a heads up to a possible delay and subtly puts Beatrice in the hot seat. In this way, Ian has enlisted her in the upgrade and publicized the role to the owners. If the meeting doesn't occur as scheduled, Beatrice's uncooperative control and block of the implementation is evident.

How to Stop a Complicator Employee

When the Complicators are your direct reports, their aversion to change hurts the success of programs and the culture. As the self-appointed historians and resident critics, they delay or destroy the opportunity to vet and implement innovations. Telling Complicators that their criticism and fault-finding is negatively affecting growth, the team, or new designs while disrupting workflow won't stop them. Delaying and blocking is their way to stay in control and maintain stability. Instead, *reduce speed, respect effort, and upgrade.*

Critical Carl

A local city wants to attract new businesses for economic development and make it easier for citizens to use services. The city's new strategic initiative states every department is to lead innovation and create new ways of delivering customer-focused service to the community. Juan is the leader of the city's information technology (IT) team. Juan's team, including several new hires, is tasked to drive this innovation. Once a week, Juan's team meets to determine the best way to serve its corporate and private citizens. When Carl attends, his questions and criticism shut down suggestions, especially from the junior members of the group. Today, another developer suggested a change to a program Carl created years ago. Carl protested, saying:

"Jessica's suggestion won't work. We've tried at least two similar approaches, and they failed miserably. As I've said during the past three months, people need to use the systems in place. When I designed the program years ago, I addressed every concern. People talk about improvements in interfacing and innovation all the time. That's just a fancy way of trying to waste our time."

> ⚠ My worst Complainer is negative from the minute he walks in the door. He reminds me of a flushing toilet that keeps running and won't stop.

 U-TURN If Carl is in attendance at a meeting, nothing meaningful is accomplished. In addition to harming the success of the city's program, Carl is harming his reputation and reducing his opportunity to be heard. Any good points he makes or wisdom he offers is lost in his attacks. As his boss, Juan should work to *reduce the speed* of the change. If possible, Carl needs time to analyze and understand the proposed innovations. Juan should pull him aside and acknowledge Carl's contribution and *respect the effort* he has used to produce through the years. Next, Juan needs to enlist Carl's help to *upgrade* the ideas and modify the process.

A private conversation with Juan might sound like this:

"Carl, you know more than anyone about these systems because you helped build them. The innovation is a strategic initiative from our mayor and the council. We need to make sure we take those systems to the next level and implement the new elements the right way. I want you involved. Can you help find a way to merge our established systems with those innovations?"

To help his meetings run more effectively, Juan needs to modify the process to get more input. He needs to let everyone, especially Carl, know the new rules. Juan should start that conversation with:

"We need to hear everyone's voice in these meetings, and we need all the data points to be successful in driving the city's initiative. Moving forward, we will use a round-robin approach. That means everyone who has an idea throws it in the hat. Then, we discuss the pros and cons of every idea. Once someone voices a concern, we'll see if others agree. Senior leaders share their opinions last and only if it adds to the discussion. If I'm not at a meeting, the process remains in effect and senior leaders ensure that everyone is heard."

If Carl refuses to adhere to the new meeting structure, he'll be left out of discussions in which the real decisions get made.

 ## Turn to Management to Help Stop Complicators

When turning to management to help with a Complicator, remember to ask and answer several questions.

How Does the Company Benefit by Helping You Negotiate with a Complicator?

Complicators create confusion in the workplace, they slow down innovation, and they keep others from working at their highest levels. Complicators criticize, micromanage, and block attempts at positive change or moving forward. They delay work and withhold or control information to ensure their power.

What Do You Want the Organization to Do?

If you are a peer or a direct report, you may need help with guidance, strategy formulation, or intervention. As a leader, you want human resources (HR) or a senior manager to support your decision to act. You may want HR or a senior leader present when you coach or counsel a Complicator to show the seriousness of the offense. A leadership representative can help the conversation stay on course and can keep the Complicator from diverting the conversation. A Complicator will attempt to poke holes in your facts, dates, or exact descriptions of the behavior. He or she will come prepared with the exact wording of the rules and a list of details and questions. Come prepared with a copy of the procedures, keep language straightforward based on the company policies, and be clear in your write-up. Above all, stay calm and don't improvise or go off-script. Prepare leadership with their own documentation so that they can back any decision you make regarding disciplinary action. People in management need preparation, copies, and knowledge if you want their support in stopping the complicating behavior.

What Communication Strategies Work with Complicators?

As you plan for discussions with Complicators, remember that they want organization, predictability, and stability. When stressed, they stall, demand accuracy, use confusing language, criticize, or require unnecessary details, especially if their stress relates to a proposed change. Complicators are introverted and logical communicators. Under extreme stress, they are impatient and explode. Let your Complicators know you appreciate their knowledge and organization. Allow time for the Complicators to think through your feedback so that they can respond.

> I worked with someone who often sounded like Chicken Little, complaining about everything as if the world were going to end as a result. Our jobs are tough enough. He is no longer with the company.

Suggest Complicators seek training or coaching to develop their natural strengths in troubleshooting, project management, and planning. Also, find them resources to improve their coping skills in emotional intelligence and communication. **Remind Complicators that the process includes obtaining the thinking of others and that change is inevitable. Unless they help upgrade or fine-tune the systems, they will be left out of the knowledge loop.**

Complicators are the historians and system designers of the organization. Often, Complicators have intimate knowledge of a system that no one else ever attempted to learn. Leadership fears that they will not be able to replace Complicators or that the Complicators will block access or even sabotage the system if reprimanded. Leadership may determine their Complicators' contributions to the knowledge and systems of the organization outweigh the risks of the complaining behavior.

 ## Turn Management Around

The best way to negotiate with management for help with your Complicator is to show the confusing, complicated, time-wasting systems being used when more sophisticated, efficient solutions exist. Paint a picture of the delays and frustration your Complicators cause and how innovations that can drive the company forward are blocked.

 ### Travel Tips to Stop Complicators

Here's what you need to know before you attempt to negotiate work drama with Complicators:

Reactions. Complicators *appear* as critics, nitpickers, know-it-alls, diverters, historians, and micromanagers. They impede, obstruct, criticize, delay, and

(continued)

(continued)

complicate to maintain their version of order, certainty, logic, and stability. They are passive-aggressive and stubborn.

Reality. Complicators *want* to slow down change and block attempts to move ahead. Masters of minutiae, they complain by finding flaws in proposed plans and/or pointing out the incompetence of others. When threatened, they push for unnecessary details or facts and force others to be precise or to comply with complicated systems or exacting rules.

 It doesn't work to appeal to Complicators to be team players, change their mind, or adopt a more positive attitude.

 The best way to negotiate with Complicators is to *reduce speed, respect effort, and upgrade.*

Reduce speed. Find a way to acknowledge the intellect that went into the Complicators' systems, methods, thought processes, or designs. Complicators have a need to be correct and want to be appreciated for a specific task.

Respect effort. Complicators fear that others will discover they don't know everything. Compliment them on their current systems and respect their specific contributions.

Upgrade. Present change or new information as a logical addition or next step. To reduce defensiveness, ask Complicators for their input or to help implement the "upgrade" to make it work within the existing design.

Chapter 3

Prima Donnas

Pay Attention to Me

⚠ Pot stirrers   ⚠ Finger pointers

⚠ Gossips   ⚠ Freeloaders

⚠ Tourists   ⚠ Drama queens/kings

Spot a Prima Donna

Negotiating with Prima Donnas reminds you of approaching a curvy road where you must pay attention or risk crashing. Prima Donnas use complaints as a means to obtain visible recognition for themselves. They use an aggressive approach to satisfy their need to be admired and liked by many. Prima Donnas feel comfortable in the spotlight and often seek it to the exclusion of others. They are articulate and at ease in front of groups. Prima Donnas know how to build coalitions to promote their position, and they complain to "voice" or represent what they claim is the group's position.

Are You Negotiating with a Prima Donna?

Prima Donnas complain to seek attention. They gossip, create drama, and stir up trouble. Prima Donnas:

- always strive for the spotlight, even to the exclusion of others.
- are quick to take credit, even for others' work.
- act superior and take no blame for mistakes.
- are really expressive and dramatic in their demeanor.
- spread gossip or negative information about others.

Reactions. Prima Donnas are brash, excessive, over the top, reactionary, erratic, and dramatic. They are humorous, even when criticizing, and are creative at getting heard and noticed. Prima Donnas are good at using words, explanations, facial expressions, tones of voice, and their bodies to express their opinions. They take credit for others' work, make promises they won't deliver on, or even lie. They are procrastinators. If something goes wrong, they point fingers and claim it isn't their fault and it's out of their control.

Reality.   Prima Donnas criticize others behind their backs to position themselves more positively. If someone gets the attention they want, they are jealous and vindictive. They seek freedom from control and detail. Prima Donnas act up, make unwarranted comments, or have disproportionate responses to express themselves and be heard. They project an air of superiority and overcompensate to gain attention no matter what. When frustrated, Prima Donnas grow argumentative, try to explain themselves, and push harder to be appreciated.

Stop a Prima Donna

Actions that Don't Work with Prima Donnas:

- **Describing why their reaction is too extreme and excessive.** Prima Donnas are more concerned with being heard than being discreet and calm. They don't want to tone down their response. Quite the opposite, they want attention and a platform.

- **Putting them on the spot.** Prima Donnas seek the spotlight, but they don't want to be on the spot, answering detailed questions. They have difficulty giving logical accounts and will deflect, leave, or shut down entirely in response to aggressive behavior or questioning from others.

- **Asking them to be rational.** Asking Prima Donnas to follow the existing systems or to validate their opinions before acting or voicing disapproval doesn't work. Logical reasoning isn't the best approach with this relationship-driven personality type.

The best way to negotiate with Prima Donnas is to remember to *acknowledge, avoid getting lost in the drama, and publicize.*

- **Acknowledge.** Let them know that you observe their behavior. Describe the personal and business consequences that may result from their current actions.

- **Avoid getting lost in the drama.** Don't play their games or get caught up in the madness. Prima Donnas are in their element when they are stirring up trouble. They are comfortable with a world that revolves around them and their opinions. Stay grounded. Insist on a problem-solving approach and have them take responsibility.

- **Publicize.** Make others aware of the Prima Donna's new role or intended outcomes. Publicizing can be embarrassing if Prima Donnas don't do as they promised.

How to Stop a Prima Donna Boss

When the Prima Donna is your boss, your job is to make him or her look good. Prima Donnas want to gain favor with clients, superiors, and peers. They pretend to know answers and make unrealistic promises that their teams or employees have trouble delivering. They may not share the spotlight or give credit to the people who make their success possible. Instead, Prima Donnas complain about others' performances. They may take undue credit for others' efforts and successes. Even though a Prima Donna is your leader, you need to *acknowledge, avoid getting lost in the drama, and publicize.*

Stingy Seth

The events team at a large venue survived a tough year. One week's events included a concert, a sporting event, and a monster truck show that required unloading several tons of dirt and then removing the dirt in a turnaround of 48 hours. The planning and execution of moving large-scale staging equipment, seating, lighting, and sound required a complex preparation. Often, crews began their day at midnight to get ready for the next event.

Despite their leader Seth being absent, the team pulled together and turned out amazing results for several productions. Actually, the team didn't mind Seth being gone. When he was present, Seth caused problems, complained to them, and got in their way. Seth even created problems for the team in other departments.

At sales meetings, Seth didn't understand his team's function or capabilities, so he often misspoke or made promises his team couldn't deliver. One big show, which would have raised a large amount of revenue, was turned away because Seth made a scheduling error. Later, he blamed losing the deal on the team's lack of support and bad attitude.

During the company's annual awards ceremony, Seth's name was called as manager of the year. Seth proudly walked up, received the award, and said:

"Thanks. This year was a big challenge for me with tough deadlines, late nights, and personal difficulties. There were a lot of problems, and I wasn't always popular. This award shows that with perseverance, you can achieve anything. I didn't realize anyone else saw the sacrifices I've made. Thank you again."

Seth didn't even mention the people who worked for him. *They* were the ones who met those tough deadlines, stayed up the late nights to deal with the changes, and ran the events while Seth handled his personal difficulties.

U-TURN Seth wants to be admired and adored so much that he doesn't advocate for his team. Having a Prima Donna boss is a tricky situation. A team or employee can't stop performing and achieving results because their jobs and reputations are involved, too. Instead, you need to *acknowledge, avoid getting lost in the drama, and publicize.*

If team members let Seth's acceptance speech go unnoticed, they send a subtle message that they agree with his version of the "facts." This could be an opportunity to manage up. As an example, Marc, a senior member of the team, could *acknowledge* Seth's behavior by saying, "Seth, you and I know how hard the team worked this year, but they didn't feel recognized today." Marc needs to *avoid getting lost in the drama*, especially any justifications Seth offers. No matter what excuse Seth makes, Marc can respond, "My concern is what you do next. Why don't you send out an e-mail to the team thanking them for making you look good and copy your boss? Better yet, why don't you send the e-mail and buy lunch for everyone? I think it will improve some spirits and encourage them to help you look good in the future."

If Seth buys everyone lunch, his effort is *publicized.* If he doesn't buy lunch, the team members' negative perception of Seth goes unchallenged. This Prima Donna drama might work itself out. Leaders who don't acknowledge their people are viewed in an unfavorable light. Prima Donnas and other complaining bosses also surface when a company has a process to determine a leader's effectiveness. Worker satisfaction surveys, 360° performance assessments, and even the company grapevine reveal how teams regard their leaders.

In the future, there are ways the team can *publicize* its accomplishments and the tremendous work being done. The team might create and have clients complete an evaluation after an event. Evaluations not only measure and document performance, they also can help obtain feedback that can be shared internally. Team members can enter events in industry showcases, give tours to clients and vendors, inform their corporate communications people of success stories, and let peers in other organizations know of accomplishments through trade association functions or publications.

 I work with people who talk the good game, but don't deliver. They talk about all they know, all the connections they have, and all the great ideas they say they are going to do. Then, when it is time to accomplish something, they are nowhere to be found. I usually end up doing the work. They get all the credit and are looked to yet again. (Sigh.)

How to Stop a Prima Donna Peer

Prima Donnas who are colleagues have complaining behavior that is brash, distracting, and gossipy. Prima Donnas interrupt and treat complaining like a theatrical production. They vent, gossip, and act like divas. Prima Donnas want to feel heard and admired by their audience. "Vacationing" at other people's offices, interrupting meetings, stopping others in the hall, and acting out their latest complaint is common. You can't avoid them or ask them to honor your schedule. They don't care how much work is on your desk. Instead, *acknowledge, avoid getting lost in the drama, and publicize.*

Parked at Parker's

Last year, Sonja and Parker worked together planning and marketing a series of global conferences. During the latest company reorganization, Parker was placed on another team and given different marketing responsibilities. With fewer people, Parker is buried with work. His former team member Sonja drops by unexpectedly and interrupts him almost daily to complain and gossip about his old team. Nothing works to keep her away. In the past three months, Parker has shut his door, asked her to reschedule, and hidden in a conference room. Sonja finds him, interrupts him, and settles in for her gripe session.

One of his new team members asked Parker yesterday, "So what's up with you and Sonja? You two are always together. I thought you had a girlfriend." Now that coworkers are talking, Parker knows something has to be done.

U-TURN Sonja uses complaining to be social. She probably misses the collaboration from last year and avoids her isolation by visiting. Parker needs to *acknowledge* to Sonja that there are personal and business consequences when she vacations in his office. He needs to *refuse to get lost in her drama* or play the role of an audience member. Parker needs to *publicize* their new agreement or policy. His conversation might sound something like this:

"Sonja, I'm calling you to discuss something serious. When you come into my office to discuss our old team, bad things happen. People ask why you're there since we no longer work together. People think we aren't working. And I don't get any work done. I work hard and I can't afford the perception that I don't. Our informal visits need to end. Just now, I sent out an e-mail to my coworkers acknowledging how busy we all are. I promised to respect their time and, wherever possible, to avoid unnecessary meetings, e-mails, and discussions regarding matters that aren't a priority. I also asked them to honor that same commitment with me. I copied you and my boss on that e-mail. Since we're not working together right now, let's stop our conversations during the workday."

 My coworker chatted incessantly and wasted much of my time. I finally took the chairs out of my office so she couldn't sit down to waste time, complain, gossip, etc.

How to Stop a Prima Donna Employee

When the Prima Donnas are your direct reports, they gossip, build cliques, and seek inappropriate attention. Prima Donna employees stir up trouble to be in the spotlight. They exaggerate perceived offenses and seek public revenge. Prima Donnas intensify their efforts to be noticed when someone excludes or doesn't acknowledge them. Prima Donnas want to feel recognized and heard. The irony is, Prima Donnas' attempts to be acknowledged can backfire and their overreactions create more of a division. You can't stop Prima Donnas by using logic, putting them on the spot, or asking them to calm down. Prima Donnas care more about venting and getting attention than the bad results their behavior brings. Instead, *acknowledge, avoid getting lost in the drama, and publicize.*

Dharma the Drama Queen

Dharma works for a firm that serves as a business partner to the telecommunications industry. Dharma's firm provides services to Tom's client. In the past, Dharma worked closely with Stuart, now Tom's boss, in troubleshooting issues, solving problems, and keeping the team members in the loop. When Stuart was promoted, Tom took on his role. On several occasions, Tom has left Dharma off the e-mail communication. This lack of communication makes Dharma feel uninformed and look incompetent. Last night was the last straw. One of the members of Tom's team forwarded an e-mail from Tom regarding their key client. Dharma should have been copied. This morning, Tom, the team, and Stuart received the following e-mail from Dharma:

"Tom, when I was forwarded your last team update from someone else, I knew I had to say something. This is the *fourth* time I've been left out of important communications in the past two weeks. We're supposed to be partners and looking out for the client's best interest. How am I supposed to do my job if you intentionally keep me in the dark? If I'm held accountable for solving these issues for our client, I actually need to *know* about the issue in real time. Your behavior is unprofessional and is hurting both of our reputations. I'm tired of doing all this work and receiving no respect from you. Please start including me in the communications immediately."

U-TURN Dharma's complaining e-mail is reflective of someone who is touchy, is explosive, and needs attention. Although some of her emotions are justified, copying Tom's team and his boss on a scathing e-mail is over the top. Tom can't respond to Dharma in an e-mail with logical reasons defending himself. Likewise, crafting an equally emotional e-mail indicating that she is destroying his reputation isn't wise and won't improve the situation.

As in many companies, Dharma is working with Tom's group through another company. Although he is the leader on the project, Tom isn't her boss, so his ability to coach Dharma is limited. Tom needs to pick up the phone and call Dharma. He should *acknowledge* her feelings and her important role on the team. "Dharma, I think picking up the phone is a better way to discuss this matter. Can you tell me what is going on?" After Dharma rants a little about being left off the e-mails, Tom can say: "Taking it from your perspective, I understand your concerns. You are now added to the main distribution list. Dharma, your actions embarrassed me in front of the team and my boss."

If Dharma tries to explain her actions, Tom should not get *lost in the drama*. He can simply say, "I'm ready to move on and serve our client. Can we agree to call each other if we experience any problems in the future?"

Tom can *publicize* their conversation with a short response to the e-mail Dharma sent: "Dharma, thank you for bringing the communication oversight to my attention. As you and I discussed earlier today, the situation has been corrected. You should now be on all e-mail distribution lists regarding this client. Please call me immediately if any other issues occur."

Now, it is Tom's turn to copy all in his response. The e-mail communication problem is addressed. If Dharma continues her outbursts or communicates in a negative manner, it's her professional reputation that will be tarnished and not Tom's.

 It reminds me of being back in high school.

Turn to Management to Help Stop Prima Donnas

When turning to management to help stop Prima Donnas, remember to ask and answer several questions.

How Does the Company Benefit by Helping You Negotiate with a Prima Donna?

There are many good business reasons for asking people in management to help you negotiate with Prima Donnas. Prima Donnas are gossipers and create cliques. With Prima Donnas, other people feel intimidated, excluded, talked about, and embarrassed. Instead of accepting responsibility, Prima Donnas will point their fingers at others. Prima Donnas cause interruptions and throw others under the bus.

What Do You Want the Organization to Do?

As a leader, you want management to back your decision on disciplinary action. You may want human resources (HR) or a senior manager present when you coach or counsel a Prima

Donna. If a leadership representative does not attend, let them know that the Prima Donna might head to their offices to give a dramatic presentation replaying your discussion, including fabricated stories about what actually was said. In preparation, consider having HR practice a coaching session with you by playing the role of your Prima Donna. You want to practice for this performance.

What Communication Strategies Work with Prima Donnas?

As you plan for discussions with Prima Donnas, remember they want attention and will act out to get noticed. Prima Donnas are loud, quick-witted, and good with words. Also, they can create a scene. They are aggressive and speak their minds, even when the words hurt their position. Under stress they grow agitated, become argumentative, and want to be heard. Under extreme stress, they shut down. Suggest Prima Donnas seek training or coaching to develop their natural strengths in public speaking and social interaction. They may also need to improve coping skills in impulse control, understand the benefits of planning, and learn to better recognize their own strengths without relying on validation by others. **Remind Prima Donnas that receiving positive recognition for a job well done is better than being noticed and creating a reputation based on negative impressions.**

What Detours and Roadblocks Do You Face?

Prima Donnas are known for connecting with others. They are great actors and put on a good show. Although they make others feel small in the process, leadership may never have seen the Prima Donna act negatively. Leadership may determine that a Prima Donna's contribution and communication abilities outweigh the risk of his or her complaining behavior.

Turn Management Around

The best way to negotiate with management is to show how Prima Donnas are creating disruption and not holding themselves accountable. Reveal instances where their storytelling is actually the telling of lies. Describe objectively the acting out they are doing and the types of scenes their negative complaining creates at work and in front of clients.

Travel Tips to Stop Prima Donnas

Here's what you need to know before you attempt to negotiate work drama with Prima Donnas:

Reactions. Prima Donnas *appear* brash, excessive, over the top, reactionary, erratic, and dramatic. They are comfortable in the spotlight, often seeking it to the exclusion of others. They take humor to the extreme, take credit for others' work, make promises they won't deliver on, and sometimes even lie. Prima Donnas are good at using words, explanations, facial expressions,

(continued)

Prima Donnas

(continued)

tones of voice, and even their bodies to express their complaints.

Reality. Prima Donnas *want* you focused on them. They have a need to be heard, admired, and appreciated and to gain attention. They are procrastinators and blamers. If something goes wrong, they point fingers and claim the problem isn't their fault or that a situation is out of their control.

 It doesn't work to explain that the Prima Donnas' reactions are too extreme, to correct or challenge them in public, or to ask them to be rational.

 The best way to negotiate with Prima Donnas is to *acknowledge, avoid getting lost in the drama, and publicize.*

Acknowledge. Let them know you have observed their complaining behavior.

Avoid getting lost in the drama. Help Prima Donnas understand the bad personal and business consequences that can result if the complaining behavior continues.

Publicize. When possible, assign Prima Donnas a personal role or outcome and publicize that role or anticipated outcome to others.

Chapter 4

Controllers

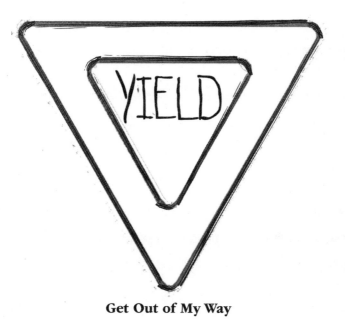

Get Out of My Way

⚡ Tyrants		⚡ Persecutors	
⚡ Demanders		⚡ Slave drivers	
⚡ Bullies		⚡ Bulldozers	

Spot a Controller

Negotiating with Controllers reminds you of yielding to a big truck coming off of a freeway ramp. Like the truck, a Controller won't stop and will run right over you if you're not careful. Controllers are aggressive, condescending, superior, challenging, impatient, intimidating, and demeaning. They are articulate, think well on their feet, and may use profanity or threatening words. Controllers are arrogant. They feel comfortable voicing frustration or "leading the attack" on you if you aren't accomplishing their desired outcome. They complain aggressively to accomplish results.

Are You Negotiating with a Controller?

A Controller uses aggressive complaining in an attempt to reach an outcome, control situations, and control people. Controllers:

- bulldoze, bully, or intimidate others.
- want to be in charge, even if not the leader.
- are avoided by others for fear of confrontation.
- interrogate and use questions to show dominance.
- enjoy making others squirm and feel uncomfortable.

Reactions. Controllers are comfortable using their bodies in an intimidating manner; this includes standing when others are seated, waving their arms, staring unnervingly at others, using a loud voice, and clutching their fists as well as pounding or throwing objects. Their tempers often escalate before calming down. After one of their abusive eruptions, Controllers expect others to mentally pick themselves up, brush off, and get back to work to get things done.

Reality. Controllers complain aggressively to accomplish their tasks and move things along. They are accustomed to being in charge and getting results. When Controllers perceive that other people are derailing a desired result or creating a roadblock, they lose patience, become more negative, and move to more forceful tactics. Their stress increases when it appears deadlines might be missed or projects will be affected. They are especially agitated when they believe that people are thwarting their efforts to move forward and achieve their own desired goal or outcome.

Stop a Controller

Actions that Don't Work with Controllers:

- **Making multiple excuses or finger pointing.** Controllers think people have the power to make things happen. If you avoid responsibility or don't admit to your mistakes, it aggravates a Controller.

- **Giving a detailed account of what went wrong.** Controllers don't want an exhaustive explanation of how the problem occurred. Controllers want a short understanding of the issue followed by a proposed solution, or preferably, two or three solutions that they can choose from and then direct the action.

- **Engaging in an aggressive counter defense.** Don't try to match Controllers in voice or body demeanor. Most Controllers are comfortable in verbal combat. They welcome the opportunity to engage and will probably win.

 The best way to negotiate with Controllers is to *stand, deliver, and let them decide.*

- **Stand.** Because of their confrontational style, your first impulse may be to avoid or hide from Controllers. Don't. Be ready to stand your ground. Be assertive and confident but not aggressive when you respond.

- **Deliver.** Deliver solutions. Let Controllers know that you hear the problems or challenges and that a plan is in place to fix the situation.

- **Let them decide.** Give Controllers the opportunity to make a decision from a short selection of options acceptable to you.

How to Stop a Controller Boss

When a Controller is your boss, you need to be ready to provide answers, show progress, and show that projects are being completed. When a Controller boss complains, he or she uses demanding questions, bullying, a loud voice, noises, name-calling, and threatening behavior. Controllers complain and use threatening language to scare and "motivate" others to act. Employees are intimidated and feel that their jobs are on the line or retribution will occur if they don't answer correctly or give the Controllers precisely what they are demanding. Don't avoid, hide, make excuses, or argue. Justifications won't work with these bullies and demanders. Instead, *stand, deliver, and let them decide.*

The Banging Boss

Crash! That sounds like something hit the wall. *Bang!* It sounds like a door was thrown open. *Bam!* Were files just slammed on a desk?

"Where the @$#! is Taylor?! I can't believe she screwed up again. It's amazing I pay people who only want to ruin my business!"

Stefan is on a tear. Unfortunately, these outbursts aren't unusual in this oil and gas company. Employees have learned that if Stefan's current ranting doesn't involve them, it's best to keep quiet, avoid eye contact, and even disappear. If you're the unfortunate soul Stefan is interrogating, you'd better give the right answers during questioning. If not, you can lose your job. It looks like Taylor is Stefan's next victim.

U-TURN Taylor needs to *stand* her ground. She needs to be calm and confident when responding to Stefan, *delivering* a solution if she has one or a plan to reach a solution that involves taking action. Then, she should have Stefan *decide* how to proceed next.

Taylor might come to the door and say, "Stefan, I'm in here. What's the issue?" If she knows the answers to his questions, she can reply, "Here's why we decided to move in that direction. Do we need to change?"

If Taylor has no answer that would satisfy Stefan, she needs time to investigate. She can tell Stefan, "The answer is I don't know. But I'll find out your options before lunch. When do you want to meet to decide, at noon or at 2 PM?"

> She drops F-bombs and other choice words depending upon her mood. Management has made little attempt to remedy the situation. We are all looking forward to her retirement in two years.

How to Stop a Controller Peer

When the Controllers are your peers, their complaining behavior includes persecuting, demanding, bullying, and generalizing, plus the use of abrasive words and intimidating actions. When Controller coworkers believe that peers are derailing their results, creating roadblocks, or making them look bad, they complain like they are in charge. They may assert tenure, expertise, relationships, or knowledge to intimidate their coworkers. Controllers lose patience and then become negative, start bossing people around, and move to a confrontational style to get things done. Do not make excuses about the lack of direction or poor communication or try to appeal to Controller coworkers' empathy. Avoiding or arguing won't work. Instead, *stand, deliver, and let them decide.*

Martha the Starter

Louis recently joined the logistics and transportation division. In his company, most of the work teams are organized in a matrix reporting structure. Everybody works together to accomplish a project with little direction or interference from management. Louis frequently needs to consult with Martha, the senior staff person on the team, to drive direction on his project. Martha can be cruel and a bully.

Today, Martha told Louis, "Louis, we need you to pull your weight. We're buried, and we should have received your numbers a long time ago."

Martha's comments are offensive, but they have some truth. Louis has not provided the data Martha requested. Part of the problem is that Martha intimidates Louis. When he joined the team a few weeks ago, he was given no clear direction, and he's afraid of making a mistake. Also, Louis doesn't want Martha to think he's stupid if he asks her to sit down with him to discuss the project.

U-TURN Louis needs to *stand* his ground. He needs to be assertive when he talks to Martha so that he can get what he needs. Louis should *deliver* a solution if he has one or the plan to reach a solution if he doesn't have an immediate answer. He needs to provide Martha with options so that she can *decide* how to proceed next.

Louis should then set up an appointment with Martha, "To discuss several matters so that the work stays on track." At the appointment, he might start with a few good, brief questions to get some direction. For example, "Martha, I've met with the provider and two people from distribution, and I still need these three questions answered by you to keep this project moving forward." At the end of the conversation, if he feels confident, Louis could say, "Martha, when I know the goal, I always execute it. I should have come to see you before now. The way we just spoke makes it easier for me to give you what you want. Thank you." Louis should have the discussion, get the information he needs, and then finish that project.

> ⚡ My worst Complainer vented at everyone. She was a complete power-tripping witch.

How to Stop a Controller Employee

When the Controllers are your direct reports, their complaining behavior includes bulldozing, bullying, and intimidating to move people to action. They may try to intimidate you, their leader, so that you won't control them. Like other Controllers, Controller employees lead unnecessary attacks and create fear to drive numbers and results. They may bully other employees, service providers, and even clients. Confronting Controller employees in front of others to make them look weak won't work. It undermines their credibility, and they will turn aggressive. Explaining, reasoning, or delaying their actions doesn't allow them to get things done. Instead, *stand, deliver, and let them decide.*

Phil Factor

The teams of financial advisors were always under stress. Each quarter, high goals were set for the number of contacts, money deposited, and products sold. Phil is a high producer who was promoted to management with no leadership training. After reviewing the numbers to date, Phil lost control and yelled at his team during their meeting.

"The handwriting is on the wall. I'm warning all of you now. You have the rest of this quarter to turn these numbers around. You'd better be here at 7 AM and stay until 7 PM every night until we hit our goal. Then maybe you'll get to keep your job."

Phil left disgusted. His boss, Mia, was in the next office and overheard Phil's talk to his team.

U-TURN Phil is a manager who desperately needs leadership and management training. Although ineffective, he is probably doing the best job he knows how. His scare tactics are not the best way to motivate employees or produce long-term results. Instead, he creates an atmosphere of fear and hostility.

As his leader, Mia needs to arrange for Phil to receive the tools and training to lead well in the organization. In her coaching, she needs to *stand up* to Phil and let him know his actions aren't appropriate or getting the results he wants. Mia can *deliver* some suggestions on training as well as ways for Phil to help alleviate the fear and damage he is causing in morale. Then, Phil can *decide* whether his next best steps mean taking a communication or leadership course. He needs better "tools" to choose the best ways to reach his desired outcome, such as reaching better numbers or motivating his team, without the controlling behavior.

In addition to suggesting training, Mia's conversation with Phil might sound like this:

"Phil, I know you're trying to boost performance. That's why your comments yesterday were so confusing. You worried our new hires. We need the new advisors to like it here so they work harder. We also want them to like you so they will come to you when they're stuck. What can you say tomorrow in the meeting to alleviate some of that fear and get them back to work?"

 He reminded me of a bully that yells and berates people to make himself seem smarter.

Turn to Management to Help Stop Controllers

When turning to management to help with your Controllers, remember to ask some important questions.

How Does the Company Benefit by Helping You Negotiate with a Controller?

The good business reasons for management to help you negotiate are that Controllers are bullies. They are the harassers of the workplace. Not only does morale and production go down when people feel intimidated, eventually most people get tired of being bullied. That means that your top performers will leave and go work elsewhere. Creativity shuts down. People who feel victimized go seek "help" in leveling the playing field. Sometimes they find help internally with other leaders and human resources. Other times, they look for help externally—including attorneys, governmental agencies, and, at times, the press—to assist them in speaking up against the bully in a powerful way.

What Do You Want the Organization to Do?

Controllers are intimidating and confident. They have no problem debating their behavior with you or approaching higher levels in the organization to protest your disciplinary action. As a leader, decide what message you want to send. Show your Controllers that you aren't intimidated by them by conducting the conversation alone. Or have human resources (HR) or a senior manager present when you coach or counsel a Controller to show you have strength and support. Prepare your senior leaders and HR that the Controller wants to be in charge. He or she may come steamrolling into their offices and they should be prepared for a show of power, intimidation, or to be bullied. You want them to assertively back you up and let your Controller know that the company agrees with you and supports putting an end to the controlling behavior.

What Communication Strategies Work with Controllers?

As you plan for discussions with Controllers, remember they want to get things done and will run over people in the process. Controllers can intimidate others with loud voices, gestures, and pointed questions. When Controllers go on the attack, they may escalate before they calm down. They are aggressive, impatient, and may explode. Under extreme stress, they can grow silent and shut down. Suggest Controllers seek training or coaching to develop their natural strengths in negotiations, leadership, and risk taking and to improve coping skills related to patience, sensitivity, and trusting others. **As the leader, you have to remind Controllers that you are the boss and that to get things done, Controllers need people *willing* to do them.**

What Detours and Roadblocks Do You Face?

Controllers are known for their confidence and for getting things done. Production and meeting deadlines are valued in most organizations. Controllers are often the leaders or will take on a leadership role. Although they often steamroll others in the process, leadership may determine that their contribution of making things happen outweighs the risk of their complaining behavior.

Turn Management Around

The best way to negotiate with management for help with Controllers is to point out the risks associated with Controllers' behavior. Show statistics of employment lawsuits, explain that the slave-driver attitude creates resentment, and give details of high performers who are affected by the bullying behavior. Discuss how employees won't speak up, feel demeaned, and are avoiding work. Describe how the confidence and need for control has harmed an important business relationship or steered a project off course. Explain that although Controllers may have a short-term gain in results, these results can't be maintained over the long term.

 ## Travel Tips to Stop Controllers

Here's what you need to know before you attempt to negotiate work drama with Controllers:

Reactions. Controllers *appear* to be tyrants, demanders, bullies, persecutors, slave drivers, and bulldozers. They are aggressive, impatient, intimidating, demeaning, and arrogant.

Reality. Controllers *want* you to yield to their authority and will run over you if you let them. They are aggressive and push hard to overcome obstacles and get results.

(continued)

(*continued*)
Controllers use complaining to get things done, motivate others to action, or get rid of restraints.

 You can't use excuses, finger pointing, detailed accounts of what went wrong, or aggressive counter defensive arguments when negotiating with Controllers.

 The best way to negotiate with Controllers is to *stand, deliver, and let them decide.*

Stand. Stand your ground. Be assertive and confident but not antagonistic when you respond.

Deliver. Let Controllers know that you heard the problems or challenges and that a plan is in place to fix the situation.

Let them decide. When possible, give Controllers the opportunity to make a decision from a narrow selection of options. They like to make decisions, especially if it means that a project will move forward or a result will be achieved.

Stop Complainers and Energy Drainers

Chapter 5

Toxics

Hazardous to Your Health

⚡ Narcissists   ⚡ Puppeteers

⚡ Egocentrics   ⚡ Borderline

⚡ Whack-a-doodles   ⚡ Sociopaths

Spot a Toxic

When you're negotiating with a Toxic personality, it is like being too close to an electric fence or poisonous material: it can be hazardous to your health. Toxic behavior is attributed to those self-absorbed people who concentrate on preserving or furthering their self-interests. They use complaining to control their environment and support their own interests. They blend into society and adapt to different social situations. Toxics like pulling strings, creating confusion, and then using the disorder or misperception to further their agendas. Toxics use this misrepresentation to deceive others. They are comfortable in chaos and often create turmoil. Toxics don't think of others unless it is how to use them to get ahead.

Are You Negotiating with a Toxic?

Toxics are dangerous individuals who complain and use misinformation to manipulate and poison the environment to further their self-absorbed agendas. Toxics:

- are deceitful, deceptive, and charming.
- twist information and present it in a fraudulent manner.
- manipulate and enjoy turmoil, drama, and chaos.
- exploit and corrupt work teams.
- are passive-aggressive and have no empathy for others.

 Reactions. Toxics may have untreated emotional problems or psychological issues, such as bipolar disorder, borderline personality disorder, or narcissistic tendencies. They are charming and disarming. Toxics can be aggressive individuals who thrive on misrepresentation and pretense. Or, they can be passive emotional roller coasters who are depressive, anxious, or distrustful of others.

Reality. Toxics use a variety of approaches to advance their egocentric needs. They aren't team players. They think of themselves, their own well-being, and how to further promote their agendas. Toxics use misinformation, corruption, distortion, fraud, exploitation, dishonesty, and poisoning of the environment to further their own self-centered needs. Toxics use complaining to promote their own interests.

Although approximately 25 percent of the population experiences some form of diagnosable mental disorder in the span of a year, Toxics make up the approximately 4 percent of the sample management population who have no conscience compared with the general population at large.[1] They are as deceitful, deceptive, corruptive, ruthless, and dishonest as needed to further their self-interests. They lack empathy or feelings of affection for animals or people. They do not consider other people's needs unless satisfying those needs helps preserve or promote their own well-being or status. **Beware.**

Stop a Toxic

Actions that Don't Work with Toxics:

- **Describing why their reaction is unproductive or causing problems with coworkers.** Toxics care about one thing: themselves. They don't care what other people think or the trouble they cause others. Toxics think only about another's opinion when that person can improve their status or diminish a threat to them.

- **Questioning or coaching them so that they can understand the fault in their approach.** Toxics don't find fault in their actions. Most have strategized the best tactics to move them ahead. They won't own a problem.

- **Appealing to their ethics or sense of doing right.** Toxics aren't troubled by society's moral values when they choose their actions. Their lack of concern for others enables them to act and achieve results, often without conscience or regret.

The best way to negotiate with Toxics is to *protect yourself, watch, and steer clear.*

- **Protect yourself.** Recognize that you aren't crazy. Remind yourself that you are a rational person who makes good decisions and has been able to get along with coworkers, bosses, and everyone else until you met this Toxic person. Set up an appointment with a counselor or executive coach. You need an expert to validate your feelings, alleviate concerns about your sanity, and offer specific suggestions about how to handle the Toxic situation.

- **Watch.** Watch how others interact with the Toxic person and who gets successful results. You may need to go to human resources (HR) and/or create your own file to document the Toxic's behavior. Keep these notes at home. Determine whom in your circle of confidants you can trust in discussing this situation or use a professional, such as an attorney, an HR professional, or an executive coach.

- **Steer clear.** Use stealth when determining your options and best course of action. If Toxics think that you are plotting against them, they may attempt to retaliate and harm your professional reputation. Keep in mind that

Toxics are masters of deception. Their drive can make them look like superstars to an organization's leadership.

Steer Clear Strategy Questions

Here are some questions to determine your best course of action in negotiating with a Toxic. Ask yourself:

Do others in leadership have any idea about the behavior or the damage being created?

Do I have a champion at a higher management level than the Toxic who would believe me?

Has our HR department been effective in responding to problems like this in the past?

What is the Toxic's history and/or reputation?

Can I negotiate my way onto another team?

What options are there to find a different position internally or outside the company?

What have others in my situation tried that has worked?

How to Stop a Toxic Boss

When a Toxic is your boss, the experience is awful. You probably won't be able to identify the reasons behind the Toxic's actions, but you can observe what works when negotiating with him or her and who gets the best results. Toxics' complaining behavior is meant to bully, divert attention from their inadequacies, misrepresent their expertise, and poison the environment to promote their interests. Toxics are interested in furthering their self-centered needs. If they don't accomplish what they say they will, they use complaining to confuse the situation and blame others for the lack of results. Don't try to reason with a Toxic boss or get on his or her good side. Instead, *protect yourself, watch, and steer clear.*

Mayor of Mayhem

A plastics manufacturer hired Jack as its new operations manager to improve the company's bottom line. In Jack's interview, he discussed the quality controls and tight operational system he implemented for his previous two employers. Jack's outcomes sounded great; they just weren't true. Unfortunately, no one checked with his former employers or the manufacturer's hiring team. If people had checked, they would have learned that the only result Jack manufactured was turmoil.

Jack started complaining about other employees on his first day. He blamed the low return on their failure to implement his productivity policies correctly. Jack gripes at meetings and torments others to hide the fact that his systems aren't helping the company's profits. His presence has poisoned the company culture. The office filled with well-functioning teammates who joked good-naturedly and celebrated special occasions became a morgue when Jack joined. Behind his back, people discuss the mayhem Jack is causing. To his face, people are professional but cautious. His biting criticism resulted in the termination of one of the most liked client services managers and, later, the forced resignation of a long-term assistant.

Jack's latest target is Christy. Jack had complained to others that he thought Christy was too happy and talkative. As she was dropping off forms today in his office, Jack said to her:

"Christy, no one is that upbeat and positive all the time. You talk too much, and I think you're faking it. I hate people who aren't authentic. Cut out the pretend cheerfulness right now and take a more professional approach, or you can cheerfully find another job."

U-TURN Christy should reassure herself that she isn't crazy and *protect herself.* She needs to *watch* all the conversations she has with Jack and also watch who is effective with him. Christy needs to formulate strategies for coping, be assertive without being aggressive, and *steer clear* of Jack's wrath when she can. Her cheerfulness needs to stop in Jack's presence.

Christy should say to Jack, "Okay. I'll alter that behavior the best I can if you think it's destructive." Then, she needs to follow up in the next week and say, "I'm following up. Have you seen any more of the destructive behavior? Is there anything else I'm doing that is bugging you?" Later, if she receives a negative performance review without having additional feedback, she can say, "Jack, this doesn't make sense. I asked you for feedback about any behavior that was bothering you. You haven't given me anything despite my requesting it." She's also ready to go to HR. When Jack gives her a project or instruction, Christy should reply in a neutral manner, stick with the facts, and stay cool, calm, and in control.

It wouldn't hurt Christy to update her résumé at home and ask those in her circle if there is an opening that would be a fit for her skill set. Christy's search takes diplomacy, speed, and an ability to use stealth. If Jack discovers her attempt to leave, he may try to retaliate.

 I suspect that these people could spot me a mile away and sought me out as a willing co-conspirator or, at the very least, a willing victim.

How to Stop a Toxic Peer

If you have Toxic peers, there is an increased likelihood of them trying to damage your reputation by making you look stupid or uninformed. Toxics use others to raise concerns or forward a risky agenda without facing the backlash themselves if the idea isn't accepted. Toxics' complaining behavior includes deceit, dishonesty, and misrepresentation to promote their self-interests. Even when Toxic coworkers appear to be your friends, you can't trust them. Don't rely on what they say. Do your own research and formulate your individual opinions independent of Toxics' words. Instead, *protect yourself, watch, and steer clear.*

Jerry the Jerk

Ross joined the general contracting firm last month as an estimator. Since his arrival, Jerry, a project manager, complained to him about the poor performance of an electrical contractor who was proposed for their next building. Over lunch one day, Jerry and Ross strategized about how to raise the issue in the upcoming preconstruction meeting. Jerry shared his thoughts with Ross:

"Look. We can't get stuck with that contractor again. His people are lazy. He doesn't know a thing about electrical installation, and he never schedules correctly. Here's what we'll do. When we get to the discussion about the subs, you question why the contractor was selected. The general manager likes to hear from the new people. When you raise the issue, it shows him you're taking initiative. You can do your 'estimating thing' and ask about criteria, competitive bids, etc. Then I'll chime in about the poor performance on his past two jobs. I'll get the other guys to talk about their experience, too. Hopefully, none of us will be forced to deal with this loser again."

In the preconstruction meeting, newcomer Ross voiced the concerns as planned about the electrical contractor. When Ross began questioning the standards for the contractor's selection, the general manager got red in the face and stopped him, noticeably furious. He told Ross he was tired of people questioning his judgment and everyone needed to lay off that electrical contractor right now. Ross looked to Jerry for support. Jerry just shrugged and smiled. No one else spoke up or made eye contact. Ross felt as if he had just been thrown under a moving bus.

Leaving the meeting, one of the other project managers patted Ross on the back and said, "Well, I guess Jerry snared you, too. I bet he didn't tell you that once you hit a precon meeting, it means the contractors are set in stone. He also probably left out that our GM and this electrical guy have been friends since high school. Well, you're not alone. Jerry 'coached' Laura to show initiative and she almost lost her job a few months ago. We call ourselves Jerry's speed bump victims. Welcome to the club."

94

Stop Complainers and Energy Drainers

U-TURN His coworker reassured Ross that he's not crazy. Ross needs to *protect himself.* He needs to *watch* all the conversations he has with Jerry. Also, the team can let Ross know what tricks Jerry might try. This can include other ways Jerry sabotages, the leadership's perception of Jerry, and what strategies work to stop him. Ross needs to let Jerry know he's on to him, and then Ross needs to *steer clear.*

Ross's conversation may go like this: "Jerry, you threw me under the bus today at the meeting. You didn't speak up as we agreed, and you knew the boss has a strong relationship with the contractor. That's not how professionals get things done." Jerry will probably lie, but at least Ross has let Jerry know that he has blown his cover for the future.

> This person would complain when he didn't get his way. He always felt his own opinion was superior to everyone else's, even the supervisor's! He had an inappropriately high opinion of his quality of work and level of skill/ability, with an equally inflated ego covered by a very soft skin.

How to Stop a Toxic Employee

When you have a Toxic direct report, that person will try to earn your trust by pretending to be your friend and sharing confidences, which may be lies. Usually, Toxics are manipulating others as well as you. Toxic employees use complaining to pull strings, misdirect, and create gossip. Toxics are charming and deceitful. They lie and twist facts to trap others and promote their own agendas. Avoid sharing feelings or any personal insights with Toxics because they will try to twist or manipulate them. Do not give any confidential or sensitive information that Toxics can use against you or others. Instead, *protect yourself, watch, and steer clear.*

Helpful Helen

Leslie is the new director of a college department. She manages several professors and support staff. Leslie was called into the university's HR office to discuss complaints filed against one of her professors, Helen. HR informed Leslie that Helen had three complaints filed against her for being unprofessional, being disrespectful to students, and gossiping about peers. HR wanted to know if Leslie had any insight. Leslie told HR that this was the first she had heard of any complaints but that she would speak to Helen about them.

As she left the HR office, Leslie thought, "There are three complaints against Helen? That doesn't make sense. Helen's *not* a gossip. She's always been super helpful to me and I trust her."

Leslie reflected on her experience with Helen. Helen had been her friend and confidant since Leslie joined the college a month ago. Helen came by to welcome Leslie and make sure she knew her way around. Helen offered to fill Leslie in on the campus politics to save her some "battle wounds." And Helen shared some of the dynamics between the professors in the department. Helen's help and insight was invaluable. She even let Leslie know when some of her department professors, especially David, were questioning her credentials and some of the policies she wanted to change.

As she was heading to Helen's office to inform her of the complaint, Leslie overheard Helen in the hall. She was badmouthing Leslie and Leslie's leadership to David. Then it dawned on Leslie, "Maybe Helen isn't so helpful after all."

U-TURN Now that Leslie has heard Helen's gossip, she knows that the complaints aren't crazy. She needs to work with HR to develop a coaching plan for Helen. She may also seek a mentor or an executive coach to *protect herself* and help her be a better chair. As Helen's manager, Leslie needs to *watch* all the conversations she has with Helen. When she responds to HR regarding her conversation with Helen, Leslie needs to let them know that she has informed Helen that gossiping and unprofessional behavior are not tolerated and that Helen needs to keep all future conversations professional. As her supervisor, Leslie can't avoid Helen, but she can *steer clear* of sharing any confidences with her or listening to her gossip.

Leslie needs to call Helen into her office and say:

"Helen, human resources wanted to see me about a situation in the office. Several complaints have been filed against you for being unprofessional and gossiping about coworkers. Why do you think people would file those complaints?"

Leslie should be prepared for Helen to deny the actions or shift the blame. If Helen does lie, Leslie can respond:

"I know there's some truth to this. I overheard you today talking in the hall about me as well. Helen, what result are you hoping to gain by talking about other people? You need to formally respond to the complaints that HR has in its office. I am reminding you to keep your conversations professional. Are you willing to do that?"

With this response, Leslie lays the groundwork for future conversations and lets Helen know she is on to her. Now, Helen knows that she has been discovered to be lying. Leslie has to be sure to talk to Helen each time she witnesses or learns of Toxic behavior. Leslie can't back down. She needs to remember there is a high likelihood that any comments Leslie makes may be repeated by Helen to others. And, if Helen can't manage to keep her conversations and actions professional, Leslie needs to manage Helen out of that position and the college.

 She is a typical narcissistic person. She is blind to anyone but herself. She seems to want attention from anyone she perceives as having some status. Recognition from coworkers doesn't matter. She often skips management levels to try to have any association, even a negative one, with upper management . . . even to the point of cornering executives in the hallway.

Turn to Management to Help Stop Toxics

When turning to management to help with Toxics, remember to ask and answer several questions.

How Does the Company Benefit by Helping You Negotiate with a Toxic?

The main business reason for management to help you negotiate with a Toxic is that Toxics poison their work environments. They are promoting their own interests, not those of the company. Toxics lack a conscience, and a company can't afford to have people without morals or consideration for others making decisions.

What Do You Want the Organization to Do?

As a leader, you may want HR or a senior manager present when you coach or counsel a Toxic. Toxics are manipulative and clever. You might want a second source to observe behaviors so that you can compare notes later. At a minimum, you want leadership to acknowledge the Toxic employee's behavior and agree that it must stop.

What Communication Strategies Work with Toxics?

As you plan for discussions with Toxics, remember they have no conscience. Toxics create confusion by using psychological warfare and empathy to further their own agendas. They are passive-aggressive and break trust over and over again. If Toxics advance, they must take advantage of and try to remain in that position because their behavior and reputation probably prevent them from working anywhere else in the company. Any communication type can be a Toxic. Toxics have been conditioned away from their natural interactional style. Extroverts are generally more visible and the introverts more covert in the way they use Toxic tactics. In the extreme, Toxics are sociopaths.

As the leader, you must reprimand Toxics on every instance of misbehavior. Stay calm and let them know that you are closely watching and monitoring everything they do. If they can't be managed to follow the plan and expectations of the job, manage them out. **Remind Toxics that developing their natural strengths in planning or strategy and**

improving skills related to sensitivity and maintaining others' trust will help them achieve their individual goals. If you send a Toxic to an executive coach, it would be very beneficial if the coach has a background in psychology. In addition, you must stay in close contact with the coach to give examples of behavior and to make sure that the Toxic hasn't charmed and fooled him or her.

Some research suggests that with Toxics' intelligence, strategic skills, and strong desire to accomplish, they can be managed as individual contributors on projects. The theory is that by keeping assignments short and high profile, Toxics won't have time to "damage" others. This drive to look good might make them less likely to turn on teammates or those who report to them.

Really?! Well, you can also keep other dangerous things around. For instance, you could put rattlesnakes in your basement to solve a rodent problem. But eventually the snakes, like the Toxics, run out of rats or projects. Then, when least expected, both start looking for other things to destroy, namely, the people upstairs, including you.

> ⚠ He poisoned the entire team. He reminded me of a snake in the grass, slithering from spot to spot, striking when no one noticed, and leaving rotting destruction in his path.

What Detours and Roadblocks Do You Face?

Toxics are known for being masterminds. They are often charming and appear to get results. They can adapt their behavior to please the people at the top while creating turmoil for others. Members of leadership may see only this charming front and be surprised that you want to write up one of the organization's top producers.

U-TURN Turn Management Around

The best way to negotiate with management for help with your Toxic is to show them specific instances where the Toxic has created turmoil. For example, show which coworker or direct report left the organization due to the Toxic's conduct. Show what isn't working because of the Toxic behavior. Discuss where the Toxic is creating problems that never existed before.

 Travel Tips to Stop Toxics

Here's what you need to know before you attempt to negotiate work drama with Toxics:

Reactions. Toxics *appear* as narcissists, psychopaths, puppeteers, poisoners, sociopaths, criminals, and "whack-a-doodles"—or people who just need mental help. They are deceitful, deceptive, ruthless, and impatient. Toxics are charming and disarming. They are intelligent and can adapt their behavior to please management while tormenting coworkers and direct reports.

(continued)

(continued)

Reality. Toxics *want* to disarm you and gain control. They are self-absorbed egotists who thrive on misrepresentation, pretenses, and fraud. They are hazardous to your health.

 It doesn't work to tell Toxics why their reactions are unproductive or causing problems with coworkers, to show them the fault in their approach, or to appeal to their ethics.

 The best way to negotiate with Toxics is to *protect yourself, watch, and steer clear.*

Protect yourself. Remind yourself that you are a rational person who makes good business decisions and has good working relationships. Get a counselor or business coach to advise you on the disorder and help you decide on your next steps. Go to HR or a champion at work.

Watch. Observe and copy responses and behavior that work and identify who successfully deals with the Toxic. Create your own file about events and conversations. Determine whether leaders respect the Toxic. Determine whom you can trust to discuss the situation.

Steer clear. Use stealth as you determine your options and best course of action. If Toxics think you are plotting against them, they may attempt to retaliate and harm your professional reputation. Keep in mind that Toxics are masters of deception.

Chapter 6

What to Do If You're the Complainer

Choose Another Route

 Whiners    Controllers

 Complicators    Toxics

 Prima Donnas    Combination

Spot Yourself Complaining

Reading through this book you may realize, "I don't *have* a Complainer . . . I *am* the Complainer." Sometimes people see themselves when they start looking specifically at Complainers and their impact in the workplace. Maybe someone gave this book to you and asked you to read this chapter. Could *you* be the problem at work? If you're a Complainer, you're putting a lot of energy and attention into addressing problems—you're just heading the wrong way.

Are You a Complainer?

Complainers use a variety of complaining styles to cope with issues and problems. Take a look at your behavior and see if any of these traits are familiar. If you feel you complain too often, you may:

- vent while people leave the room or ignore you.
- whine, gripe, or even withdraw to get attention.
- complicate matters, nitpick others' ideas, or frustrate people in meetings.
- gossip about coworkers or increase stress by over-reacting.
- explode or intimidate others.
- not be trusted by others or not given confidential information.

Reaction. You may have received feedback that you are complaining or not interacting professionally. Have you been excluded from a meeting, a project, a key assignment, or even a team outing? Ever catch yourself interrupting others, talking negatively about coworkers, or feeling happy when someone else makes a mistake? Have you lost your temper, felt frustrated with coworkers, or withdrawn from conversations? Maybe you feel helpless or that others are blocking you from completing important work?

If you think you are complaining too much, which behavior sounds like yours? Are you using an aggressive approach to get things done or be noticed? Are you more passive in order to be connected or receive empathy? Are you using passive-aggressive behavior in an attempt to control an environment or shake things up? Or do you find yourself combining several of the complaining types?

Reality. There are many reasons you're complaining. *Take note*, because this behavior is damaging to your professional reputation. Why are you complaining? Are you overworked? Do you feel like you don't have control over your outcomes? Are you experiencing health problems or family demands that are creating stress?

You could have a coping strategy that worked for you when you were growing up, but no longer serves you as a working adult. Do you have any limiting beliefs or self-defeating behaviors that are holding you back? You might have unresolved issues from your past that are surfacing and sabotaging you now. Did you even know you were complaining or that you were doing it so much? Often, your worst critic is living in your head. Do you consider yourself worthy of success? Are you putting unreasonable expectations on yourself? Maybe you are in a job that is not your passion, your work doesn't match your skills, you need more training, or leaders aren't giving you direction and feedback. There are better ways to get things done than complaining.

Take the free online assessment "Are You Seen as a Complainer?" at www.StopComplainers.com.

Which Complaining Behaviors Am I Using?

When you are under stress, which complaining behavior best describes you and the need you are trying to meet?

- **Whiner:** Do I feel better when others understand my problems?

- **Complicator:** Do I dislike change or when things are not stable?

- **Prima Donna:** Am I complaining so that others will notice all the work I'm doing?

- **Controller:** Am I trying to gain control of chaotic situations because this work *needs* to get done?

- **Toxic:** Do I stir the pot or shake people up a little so that I can further my own agenda?

Under stress, most of us exhibit these types of complaining behaviors and sometimes more than one. Surprisingly, some people say they don't complain at all and won't tolerate Complainers.

According to the survey, the top reasons people complain at work are: unclear direction, lack of feedback from leadership, incompetent coworkers or boss, unrealistic demands from others, and too much work.

What Are They Complaining About?

Answer	0%　　　　　　　　　　　100%	Number of Responses	Response Ratio
Job fear and/or pressure to perform	▄	143	14.2%
Unclear direction or lack of feedback from leadership	▄▄▄▄▄	445	44.4%
Too much work to do	▄▄▄	278	27.7%
Deadlines	▪	91	9.0%
Reorganization or change in work environment	▄	122	12.1%
New boss	▏	12	1.1%
Unrealistic demands from clients or customers	▄▄▄	286	28.5%
Incompetent vendors, suppliers or contractors	▄	133	13.2%
Incompetent coworkers or boss	▄▄▄	312	31.1%
Inadequate pay or benefits	▪	88	8.7%
Health issues	▏	42	4.1%
Personal or family issues	▄	113	11.2%
Not feeling heard or respected at work	▄▄▄	260	25.9%
Just feels good to vent or let off steam	▪	94	9.3%
Being micromanaged	▄▄	224	22.3%
Disagreements with coworkers	▪	64	6.3%
Other	▪	72	7.1%
Totals		**1000**	**100%**

Note: Other included "I don't complain," "Unethical business dealings and unprofessional behavior," "financial pressures," "duplication of efforts," and "I'm pleading the Fifth."

Spot Yourself Complaining

Actions that Don't Work:

- **Complaining with no action.** Stop ignoring the issue, blaming others, or continually venting and creating stress. The more you gripe about problems, the larger they grow (at least in your mind) and the more people you repel in the process.

- **Repeating the same actions.** Don't use broken strategies. For example, relying on others for an emotional "fix" cripples your future success.

- **Continuing to chastise.** Beating yourself up is unproductive, adds additional stress, and doesn't improve your behavior.

 The best way to negotiate with your complaining behavior is to *identify the issue, understand strengths, and be proactive.*

- **Identify the issue.** Admit you have a problem and that your current strategies aren't working. Ask a professional for objective feedback and an understanding of the reasons you act the way you do. Depending on the issue, contact an executive coach, a mentor, a counselor, or a psychiatric or medical professional.

- **Understand strengths.** Take an assessment and learn your talents and the value you bring. Explore self-development to learn the skills and techniques you need to take those strengths to the next level. Pursue assertiveness training, learn influence techniques, attend a communication program, and/or invest in stress management.

- **Be proactive.** Focus on the right things. Adopt a problem-solving, assertive, and proactive manner. Form supportive relationships, construct appropriate personal boundaries, and practice positive complaining and diplomacy. Instead of focusing on what your problem is, work on solving it. Talk positively and

109

encouragingly to yourself. Give yourself permission to fail and make adjustments. Contributors focus on the future, problem solving, and others. Complainers dwell on the past, their fears, and themselves.

Stop Your Complaining

Explore your reasons for complaining to curb your appetite for the wrong type of attention. Before you address the work drama you create, ask yourself these questions:

1. What need am I trying to address through my actions? (Identify the issue.)

2. Instead of complaining or creating additional problems, what strength could I contribute or develop to help this challenge? (Understand strengths.)

3. Am I proactively improving the situation or am I creating additional problems? (Be proactive.)

 Complaining begets more of the same. I have seen careers killed because of a person's complaining. Saddest thing is when they don't even realize it.

The following sections provide examples of people using complaining as a way to meet their needs. See if you can spot any similar complaining you want to stop.

How to Stop Complaining Like a Whiner

Whiners complain to form relationships and receive empathy. They vent, withdraw, and want others to solve their problems.

Are You Complaining Like a Whiner?

Whiners:

- complain about how things aren't fair.

- play the victim and are powerless.

- always seem to have something wrong in their lives.

- are always upset about something or someone.

- never bring any solutions, only problems.

If you complain like a Whiner, you moan and groan. You vent, gripe, and become frustrated with yourself and others. You pout, sulk, and withdraw. You feel overwhelmed and don't see a way out. You'll focus on the problem and the past instead of the future and solutions. Feeling sorry for yourself and dwelling on the past doesn't help. Asking others to create solutions that you have to put in place and live with doesn't make sense either. Instead, *identify the issue, understand strengths, and be proactive.*

Sad Sandy

Despite years of experience and performing many of the functions of the role, Sandy didn't apply for the new opening in management. When she got notice that a coworker, Andrew, got the job, she called a friend and said:

"Andrew is the new manager. Really?! I should have applied for that position. I just couldn't imagine leading people who were my peers. But Andrew?! He has no experience, no time with the company, nothing that I don't have . . ."

Sandy is angry and disappointed with herself. She talked herself out of applying for a job. She held herself back, and a less-qualified candidate was selected. Sandy is right. Andrew has nothing in his background that would have given him the edge over Sandy for the new job—with the exception that he actually applied. Can you relate to Sandy? Do you complain like a Whiner?

 To turn a situation like this around, you need to *identify the issue.* In Sandy's case, she needs to determine why she chose not to apply rather than focusing on who got the position. Does this sound familiar? Have you ever been afraid of rejection? Do you worry about failing at the job or not living up to expectations? Could you lack self-confidence? If so, the answer is to get a better *understanding of your strengths* and the value you bring to the company. Do you need training or coaching to feel comfortable in communication, leadership, or risk taking? *Be proactive.* How could you approach your leader and/or human resources to let them know that you want to apply for the next leadership position or growth opportunity?

> ⚠ My fear of the unknown and lack of goals makes me a Complainer.

Instead of Whining, question yourself with, "Wow. I wonder why I'm getting so emotional. This must be really important to me. I need to calm down before I act."

Break through complaining like a Whiner by reminding yourself, **"This is not life or death. If I whine, people won't want to be around me or help me."** When a future opportunity comes your way, tell yourself, "Why not me? What have I got to lose?"

How to Stop Complaining Like a Complicator

Complicators complain to avoid change and maintain stability. They frustrate, complicate, and create confusion.

Are You Complaining Like a Complicator?

Complicators:

- delay and put up roadblocks if something new is offered.

- nitpick and criticize others' work.

- bring up past failures and mistakes.

- protect systems and information.

- use knowledge and details to confuse and complicate matters.

When you complain like a Complicator, you criticize, obstruct, nitpick, confuse, and impede others. Complicators are good with a lot of information and details, but change disrupts their version of certainty, order, and stability. If you are a Complicator, you complain to block disruptions to structure, to maintain predictability, and to avoid feeling vulnerable or incompetent. Complaints are not going to block a change long-term. If you create too much of an interruption or confusion, you will be left out of important decisions and left to manage the change without input. Instead, *identify the issue, understand strengths, and be proactive.*

Change Artist Charles

Charles has the highest accuracy rate for the retail company in balancing accounts and predicting future spending. He takes large amounts of data and creates formulas to forecast trends and the direction the business is heading. Charles was told he needs to handle Trevor's job while Trevor takes a vacation. It's a standard practice for employees to cover for one another when they take any type of leave.

Trevor's job has more direct involvement with store managers. Managers call in data and discuss problems as they occur. Charles gripes about handling Trevor's job to anyone who will listen, including his family, friends, coworkers, and members of different teams. Charles's gripes include:

"This is wrong. I'm going to have to take over all of Trevor's responsibilities for two weeks. Trevor's job has all these interruptions from the managers during the day. The stores close later, so I have to stay later four nights a week to answer their questions. What's going to happen to my accuracy rate when I'm off doing someone else's work?"

Charles's anxiety is obvious. He is out of his comfort level and not using his strengths around numbers and systems. Also, he doesn't want to risk his accuracy to handle the interruptions in Trevor's position. Can you relate to Charles? Do you complain like a Complicator?

 To turn a situation like this around, you need to *identify the issue, understand strengths, and be proactive.* To be proactive in Charles's case, he could look for changes or upgrades to make to Trevor's system while Trevor is gone.

> There is always someone complaining about something. Sometimes I'm one of them.

Like Charles, take a deep breath and remind yourself that feeling uncomfortable is a temporary situation. Seek out opportunities to contribute by improving or upgrading instead of complicating. *Break through complaining like a Complicator* by reminding yourself, **"Change is inevitable. I'd rather be involved in creating a solution or upgrading the system than have no input."**

How to Stop Complaining Like a Prima Donna

Prima Donnas complain to seek attention. They pass along stories they've heard, create drama, and stir up trouble.

Are You Complaining Like a Prima Donna?

Prima Donnas:

- always strive for the spotlight, to the exclusion of others.

- are quick to take credit, even for others' work.

115

What to Do If You're the Complainer

- act superior and take no blame for mistakes.

- are expressive and dramatic in demeanor.

- spread gossip or negative information about others.

If you complain like Prima Donnas, you interrupt, ignore your job, seek self-serving attention, and make inappropriate remarks. You disrupt and create scenes. Prima Donnas want to be seen and heard. You create opportunities, even negative ones, to interact with others. Goofing off, avoiding duties, or getting negative attention are sure ways to get yourself reprimanded or fired. Instead, *identify the issue, understand strengths, and be proactive.*

Mind-numbing Math Mike

Mike's promotion isn't working. It took him away from his "fun" job in the bank: dealing with the customers. He procrastinates on his reports because they are monotonous and don't matter. Instead, he fills his time by calling his friends and chatting on online communities. Mike often leaves his office to visit the front lobby just to interact with people instead of his computer screen. Yesterday, he took a two and a half hour lunch with some old college buddies. When he returned, he talked so loudly on his cell phone that everyone, including bank customers, looked at him. Today, he was gossiping to a loan officer about not being paid what he was worth.

"The numbers are starting to blur. I hate the monthly reconciliation report and all the stupid documentation. We turn in the numbers. They send more numbers back. Nothing changes, and no one recognizes my hard work. It's confusing and so exacting. It's a horrible job. If someone offers *you* a promotion around here, don't take it. Since when did a promotion translate into boredom, no people, and no fun?"

Mike's promotion isn't a fit for him. He has recognized that someone who is great with people may not be the best fit for a job analyzing numbers. No amount of training or coaching is going to fix the fact that he's not using his strength: working with customers. Even though he likes the idea of a promotion, Mike needs to interact with people. Connecting is his strength. Mike knows he needs to act quickly before his poor performance makes it impossible for him to transfer and even cost him his job. Can you relate to Mike? Do you complain like a Prima Donna?

 To turn a situation like this around, you need to *identify the issue, understand your strengths, and be proactive.* In Mike's case, he will want to talk to his boss and see if there are other opportunities to interact with people, including returning to his old job.

> ⚠ We, alone, are responsible for our actions and feelings. No one can make us feel bad if we don't let them.

Instead of acting like a Prima Donna, remember your strength is connecting and communicating. *Break through complaining like a Prima Donna* by reminding yourself, **"If I gossip, interrupt others, or draw inappropriate**

What to Do If You're the Complainer

attention to myself, people won't see how hard I work.
I want positive, not negative, recognition."

How to Stop Complaining Like a Controller

Controllers use aggressive complaining in an attempt to reach
an outcome, to control situations, and to control people.

Are You Complaining Like a Controller?

Controllers:

- bulldoze, bully, or intimidate others.

- want to be in charge, even if not the leader.

- are avoided by others for fear of confrontation.

- interrogate and use questions to show dominance.

- enjoy making others squirm and feel uncomfortable.

When you complain like a Controller, you may use an
angry tone, throw things, or be abrupt, demanding, and loud.
Controllers like to get things done. You don't want delays, to
work with people you don't value, or to waste time. Don't
intimidate others or create fear. Instead, *identify the issue,
understand strengths, and be proactive.*

Fed Up Fred

Fred threw his computer case into his backseat, screamed an
obscenity, and slammed the door so hard the car shook. He
called his girlfriend and unloaded his complaints:

"I can't believe it takes this much time for those idi-
ots to make up their minds. No one can make a decision

around here without running it by the finance department for approval. However, no one in finance will respond to e-mails or phone calls.

"I *finally* got one of the assistants on the phone and demanded an answer out of her. I told her to just let me know if we have the budget to proceed or not. She said she'd call me back. Well, she never did. Instead, someone who works on her floor said she was crying after she spoke to me. *Crying?!* Can you believe it? We're supposed to be adults.

"Then, as I was giving my status update to my boss, he told me that my project is now a low priority. After I've spent so much time on this project, it's now a low priority?! *Are you kidding me?* I'm sick of doing these useless fire drills. Let's get *something* done that actually matters and stop wasting my time and the company's money."

Fred is frustrated. He is facing bottlenecks in obtaining approval and working on projects that are not priorities. He can't get things done, so he demands and yells at people at work *and* at his girlfriend. Fred's strengths are his dedication and willingness to put in extra effort to get things accomplished. However, his drive and need to get things done have him crushing others in the process. Can you relate to Fred? Do you complain like a Controller?

U-TURN To turn around a situation like Fred's, you need to *identify the issue*. Fred needs to determine whether it is lack of direction, working on low priorities, the inability to get approvals when he needs them, or just the constant change of concerns in business. Have you ever felt like you

What to Do If You're the Complainer

were running in molasses and couldn't get anything done? Do you ever feel like people are more of a hindrance than a help? Are people getting in the way of accomplishing work? Do you ever get impatient or lose your temper? First, you need to understand the issue that is creating that stress.

 Tasks are taking longer than I anticipated, so I have crammed an unrealistic amount of work into a limited amount of time.

Like Fred, the answer is to *understand your strengths*. Do you make decisions well and prioritize effectively? When you aren't mowing people over, are you good at motivating them? *Be proactive.* Instead of attempting to do it all alone, reach out. For instance, discuss a time issue or direction with your boss. When you ask for help, prepare for those conversations with specific examples, the areas where you are getting "stuck," and the ideas you've generated to address the issue. Then, be willing to listen to others' suggestions and feedback.

Break through complaining like a Controller by reminding yourself, **"I've got to back off and cool down. If I run over people in the process, I'll never get anything done. Leading people to *help me* make decisions *will help them* buy into solutions."**

How to Stop Complaining Like a Toxic

Toxics complain and use misinformation to manipulate the environment to further their own agendas.

Are You Complaining Like a Toxic?

Toxics know how to:

- be deceitful, deceptive, and charming.
- twist information and present it in a fraudulent manner.
- manipulate and enjoy turmoil, drama, and chaos.
- exploit and corrupt work teams.
- be passive-aggressive and have little to no empathy for others.

When you complain like a Toxic, it appears that you thrive on chaos and know how to use charm to mislead others. Toxics can complain and use misinformation to manipulate the environment and further an agenda that appears to be based on their self-interests only. Is this true for you? Do you have the ability to manipulate others, twist information, or lie? If so, this is not a good long-term strategy, and you will be discovered. Instead, *identify the issue, understand strengths, and be proactive.*

Problematic Pablo

Pablo works as the business development officer for a trade association. He is successful in attracting major sponsors for trade shows. Those who work with him know that Pablo is unpredictable—friendly one moment and then a bully the next. Pablo had a "motivation" idea while watching a reality survival show. He was impressed at how easily some of the contestants could get others to squirm and comply with crazy requests.

Pablo thought his idea would be a good motivator for the office and shake things up a bit. As an experiment, he would pit two employees against each other in a competition to determine which one could "win" a job for another year. Pablo called Brynn and Brooke, his two assistants, into his office. "I'm not happy with either of your performances right now, and you're embarrassing me in front of our leadership," Pablo complained. "The board is looking at the possibility of staff reductions, and it's likely that only one of you will be funded at the end of the year. Let's see who can do the best job and not let me down. May the best woman win."

Brynn and Brooke left the office confused. Earlier in the month, Pablo had said they were the best employees he'd had in their roles. Also, they questioned whether this was in fact a board decision, because the board doesn't meet again until later in the quarter.

Pablo is creating problems and putting people into emotional chaos. Whether the issue is boredom, lack of work challenges, or a need to control, he should identify why he is creating the turmoil. The confusion Pablo creates will not help him meet the trade association goals. If Brynn or Brooke begins asking questions of the board about his statements or if they leave to work elsewhere, his experiment may backfire and create issues for him. Can you relate to Pablo? Do you complain like a Toxic?

 U-TURN To turn situations like Pablo's around, you need to *identify the issue.* Have you ever played devil's advocate, stirred the pot a little, or manipulated a situation to see how people would react? Can you imagine creating a little turmoil to see the result? The answer to stopping Toxic behavior is to *understand your strengths* and use them to contribute to the organization instead of damaging the entity that provides your paycheck. For instance, Pablo's strengths are creativity and an ability to sell.

Once you know the issue and understand your strengths, choose to *be proactive.* In Pablo's situation, he could encourage Brynn and Brooke to help him in sales rather than frighten them with job loss. Encouraging them to help make more money is in the best interests of the association, Brynn and Brooke, and, of course, Pablo. In addition, developing ways to increase sales uses Pablo's creativity. What strengths do you have that would allow you to be proactive, yet retain creative control?

 She was like a passive-aggressive, schoolyard bully. She played mind games and used other types of intimidation and disrespect to get her way.

Break through complaining like a Toxic by reminding yourself, **"I can't burn my bridges because I don't know whose help I'll need in the future. If people don't trust me, they won't include me, do the work I need done, or put me in new roles. If I encourage others and am consistent, I'll get more of what I want."**

Why Are You Complaining?

Complaints work. However, they don't work forever. Chronic complaining just isn't a long-term business strategy for success. If you determine what drives your behavior, you can find an effective alternative. What are your reasons for complaining? Perhaps you don't know how to assertively ask for what you want. Maybe you are self-sabotaging or blocking your progress because of "baggage" or past experiences. You could have low self-confidence or lack of support or direction. Perhaps your environment is depressing, or the office politics are oppressive. Poor time management, lack of priorities, and lack of direction create stress. If you're not working in a job that plays to your strengths, you're not alone.

A September 2012 Gallup poll reports that 57 percent of American adults say they are not able to use their "strengths to do what they do best throughout the day." The report suggests that those who use their strengths are "more engaged in their work, exhibit higher performance, and are less likely to leave their organization." Gallup also reports that only "30% of US workers were engaged in their work and workplace during the first half of 2012," while 52 percent reported being "not engaged" and 18 percent "actively disengaged."[1]

Complaining is a way of satisfying unmet needs and expressing stress. Complaining also can serve as a warning that others are experiencing work drama. Psychologist

Dr. Sherry Buffington states that people complain to be valued, heard, and appreciated. Buffington says, "All actions and inactions occur in an effort to meet our deepest human need: the need to be valued, either in our own perception or in the perception of another. The most powerful management tool on Earth is the ability to see and understand the need that drives the behavior and to help the individual get that pressing need met."

According to Buffington, people fall into two camps. There are the more logical, thinking communicators who complain to increase their control, produce results, or maintain stability, and there are the more relational, feeling communicators who complain to obtain connection, reassurance, and appreciation.

 Wow. I complain a lot and can equally tick many boxes in this survey, sorry.

The irony is that the act of complaining often produces the *opposite* effect of the results both types of Complainers seek. The logical, thinking Complainers create chaos or are left out of decisions instead of receiving the control or certainty they want. And the relational, feeling Complainers are avoided and ridiculed instead of obtaining empathy or recognition.

Complainers aren't popular among coworkers or leaders. Peers resent doing good work while Complainers slack off or delay results. Leaders are judged on their poor performance. The negativity Complainers create actually causes people to quit jobs they like.

125

What to Do If You're the Complainer

What Your Coworkers Are Saying About You

Here is how people describe their complaining colleagues:

"I figure they are lonely and miserable at home so they have to come to work and make us miserable."

"They are never satisfied. They are doing just enough work to get by and enjoy having others feel the same way they do. They are able to turn a good situation into a bad situation and are not able to see the good in things."

"They think their job is just something to do when they feel like it. They are irresponsible and childish."

"They are at their worst when it is time to be accountable for a project. They complain throughout the project, trying to blame others for their lack of ownership and accountability."

"They whine incessantly and look for ways to keep things stirred up since they aren't happy."

"It is pettiness and complaining about irrelevant things or about things without the accurate information."

"Whiners tend to be people [who] are trying to get out of doing their job. By whining, they take attention away from the fact that they are either incompetent or have other problems."

"They should be reassigned or fired. If a situation is that horrible, they should move on."

Good Business Reasons to Curtail Your Complaining

Complaining is not an effective way to express yourself as a professional. No matter what type of complaining you use, from whining or griping to withdrawing or exploding, complaining limits your career opportunities. In addition, your abilities to function, think, and produce good results are negatively affected by complaining.

An expert in transition and integration, Ginger Shelhimer, LPC, SPHR, advises that Complainers limit their opportunities for growth, promotion, and even continued employment. Shelhimer states that when inevitable change occurs in organizations and choices have to be made about which employees to retain, those employees who solve problems and bring forward solutions are always more highly valued and are the focus of retention efforts rather than those who tend to complain about problems.

Good News and Breakthroughs

The good news is that you are not alone. Enlightened Complainers often choose to stop. Their breakthroughs occur for a variety of reasons. Many former Complainers report someone pointed out their complaining. Others say they discovered their natural strengths or style through an assessment, a coach, or a training program. When these "rehabilitated" Complainers began developing their talents, they knew what type of work was suitable, where they performed well, and what activities to avoid. They also learned others' motivators and communication styles, which enabled them to interact more effectively. The need for complaining went away when their uncertainty and stress were alleviated and they saw a proactive way to contribute.

Have a Breakthrough and Stop Complaining

If you would like to have a breakthrough and stop complaining, ask yourself the following:

- *If I could communicate in a way that people heard me and helped me achieve my goals, what would be possible for me in my career, in my relationships, and at home and work?*

- *How could I show up powerfully and assertively while still being diplomatic?*

- *What would the most influential person I know do in this situation?*

- *What would be the best next step to propel me forward personally and professionally?*

- *What unique strengths, gifts, and talents can I contribute and develop?*

Other reformed Complainers decided as a department or group to stop complaining. Breakthroughs often occur when management recognizes and resolves environmental issues or corrects Energy Drains that are the source of complaints. Occasionally, Complainers are promoted or transferred to jobs that require managing other Complainers. These former Complainers say that being in a customer-facing role or serving as a supervisor requires adopting a more positive attitude.

When you learn to communicate more effectively, people gravitate to you, connect with you, let down their guard, and listen to your requests.

 Travel Tips to Stop Your Complaining

Here's what you need to know before you attempt to negotiate the work drama:

 Reactions. If you *appear* as a Whiner, Complicator, Prima Donna, Controller, Toxic, or a combination of several of these types, you might be a chronic Complainer.

Reality. Try to determine what you *want* to accomplish or what need you wish to fill through your complaining. Watch your behavior and see when the complaining appears the most. Are you trying to relate with others, maintain stability, be noticed, or get things done? Are you under stress? Are you dealing with Energy Drains?

(continued)

What to Do If You're the Complainer

(continued)

  It doesn't work to complain with no solutions, to repeat ineffective actions, or to chastise yourself.

To stop complaining and start contributing, remember to *identify the issue, understand your strengths, and be proactive.*

Identify the issue. Determine Energy Drains creating stress. Acknowledge any unmet needs and admit your current coping strategies aren't working. Seek objective feedback and help, including expert opinions or medical advice.

Understand strengths. Learn your talents and value to communicate powerfully and contribute effectively. Explore self-development and training.

Be proactive. Adopt a problem-solving manner that allows you to contribute to others and your organization. Form supportive relationships, construct appropriate personal boundaries, and practice diplomacy.

Break through complaining. Remind yourself, *"I want"*:
"Supportive, not powerless, relationships." **Whiner**
"Input, not exclusion, in changes." **Complicator**
"Positive, not negative, attention." **Prima Donna**
"Lasting results, not bullied victims." **Controller**
"Trust, not suspicion, to help reach goals." **Toxic**

Chapter 7

Energy Drains

Construction Ahead

⚡ Direction/leadership   ⚡ Paperwork/scheduling

⚡ Bottlenecks/red tape   ⚡ Interruptions/meetings

⚡ Technology challenges   ⚡ Environment/culture

Spot the Energy Drains

When you are negotiating with an Energy Drain, it is like driving through a long stretch of road construction. You see workers hard at work and what looks like a mess, and you experience delays and frustrations. Energy Drains are environmental factors, organizational constraints, and systems and processes that cause unnecessary stress on employees. They are time-consuming, frustrating, and demanding.

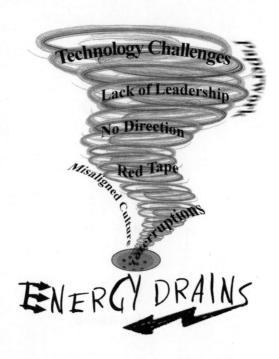

Are You Negotiating with an Energy Drain?

Energy Drains are stressful and unproductive. They stifle environments and culture through illogical methods, restrictive constraints, and complicated systems.

Energy Drains:

- make you feel powerless, helpless, and weak.

- dictate an illogical procedure, cumbersome protocol, rigid instructions, or a complex system that must be followed.

- are overwhelming, confusing, or overly complex.

- oppress work environments and culture.

- hamper productivity and contribution.

- interfere with planning, execution, and creativity.

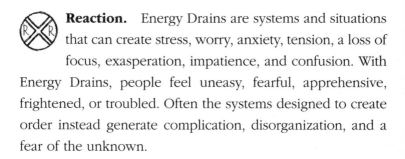 **Reaction.** Energy Drains are systems and situations that can create stress, worry, anxiety, tension, a loss of focus, exasperation, impatience, and confusion. With Energy Drains, people feel uneasy, fearful, apprehensive, frightened, or troubled. Often the systems designed to create order instead generate complication, disorganization, and a fear of the unknown.

Reality. Energy Drains involve a lack of direction, unclear expectations, and lack of guidance, transparency, or goals. They can be caused by ill-suited work, political oversight, delays, mistakes, and office politics. People describe Energy Drains as poor communication from leadership, rhetoric, over-assignment of work, lack of work, and bureaucratic policies. Energy Drains include bottlenecks such as waiting on others to do their jobs, waiting for approval, correcting the problems of others, not having defined systems, dealing with poor workflow management and inefficiencies, following policies that don't make sense, and using time-wasting, cumbersome systems.

Things that Interrupt or Drain Energy

* In addition to people, what types of things interrupt or drain your energy during the work day? Please select your top 3 only.

Answer	0% 100%	Number of Responses	Response Ratio
Technology challenges		427	42.7%
Work environment		218	21.8%
Reading and responding to e-mail, IMs, or texts		477	47.7%
Phone calls & voice messages		214	21.4%
Meetings/conference calls		351	35.1%
Company bureaucracy/red tape		359	35.9%
Bottlenecks/waiting for others to do their jobs		429	42.9%
Other		85	8.5%
	Totals	998	100%

The most commonly reported interruptions or drains on energy during the workday are: reading and responding to e-mail, IMs, or texts; dealing with technology challenges; waiting for bottlenecks to clear and for others to do their jobs; dealing with company bureaucracy/red tape; meetings; and participating in conference calls.

Stop the Energy Drains

 Actions that Don't Work When Dealing with Energy Drains:

- **Losing patience or getting exasperated or emotional.** These are systems and situations. Although created by people, Energy Drains lack emotions, and an emotional response won't fix them.

- **Ignoring or postponing them.** Most frustrations don't go away or get better on their own. Escaping an environment by calling in sick makes it appear you aren't performing. Trying to avoid the drain or living with the results it produces actually takes more energy than resolving or working around the frustrations.

- **Fighting the system or situation.** Effective change requires strategy and experience. It requires cooperation and influence, not anger.

 The best way to negotiate with Energy Drains is to *identify, control, and negotiate the rest.*

- **Identify.** Identifying the issue is the first step. What is the problem? What direction or solution makes the biggest difference, the soonest? Who else can provide input on the solution? Surely you're not the only one frustrated by this issue. Locate a roadmap of what's been tried before now.

- **Control.** Move into a problem-solving mode. Replace disorganization with systems that work and use those systems on a consistent basis. Plan each week. Block your time and assign certain activities to occur during the block. Design conference hours to help manage interruptions. Watch for patterns and plan for recurring time-consumers such as midmorning meetings, problems that arise at the same time each month, or interruptions that occur only during certain days of the week. Take yourself off of unnecessary e-mails, automate standard responses, and designate certain times of the day to respond to e-mails and voice messages. If you can't fix the challenge, control your response to it.

Days of Week You Experience Complainers or Energy Drains the Most

What day(s) of the week do you experience Complainers, interruptions or Energy Drainers the most?
❖ Please comment below why you believe this/these day(s) receive the most.

Answer	0% 100%	Number of Responses	Response Ratio
Sunday	▌	27	2.9%
Monday	████████████████	522	56.1%
Tuesday	████	209	22.4%
Wednesday	████	199	21.3%
Thursday	████	214	23.0%
Friday	████	257	27.6%
Saturday	▌	34	3.6%
Totals		**998**	**100%**

An Energy Drain you can't control is the day of the week. Not surprisingly 56.1% of people say they experience Complainers and Energy Drains the most on Mondays because, "It ends their weekend, so they come to work cranky and fired up to complain the rest of the week."

- **Negotiate the rest.** Stop the frustrations you can. Look for tasks that can be deleted or delegated. Create boundaries. Ask if the meeting or conference call is necessary. Determine if your presence is needed or if you can send a representative. Seek training and coaching where needed. In particular, borrow others' learning and discoveries without investing all the time, effort, risk, or mistakes.

How to Negotiate Energy Drains Involving Technology

Systems which force you to follow specific procedures and where you have a lack of authority to cause change are drains

> ⚠ I'm drained by reports due on Fridays about what I accomplished in the week. Well, I would accomplish a lot more if I wasn't spending 2 hours trying to summarize what I was doing all week.

of time and energy. Some have a great design in one area but create chaos in another. This is often the case when someone who has to use the system hasn't been consulted in designing the system. Instead of becoming frustrated, *identify, control, and negotiate the rest.*

Traveling Tony

Tony often has to travel for work. The new travel reimbursement policy at his company is strict. Estimated airline fees and hotel expenses are submitted before a request is approved. Unfortunately, approvals take weeks, and prices increase. To stay within the approved budget requires flight changes with layovers and inconvenient departure times. Upon return from each trip, Tony faces more obstacles. All original receipts must be submitted within 10 days or they may not be reimbursed. Each expense must be compared against the estimated line item and input at the same time because the online form can't save information. As Tony attempted to supply his most recent receipts, he became frustrated. "Enter the 15-digit number of the contract from my rental car? I kept the receipt, but I'm not sure I have the contract anymore. I spend more time on the travel reimbursement than I do on the trip. I sure hope this travel policy is saving the company a ton of money. I know none of us want to travel anymore, which is fundamental to closing new business and making more money for the company!"

U-TURN First, *identify* the problem. In this case, the Energy Drain is a cumbersome system requiring strict compliance or a penalty of no reimbursement. Then, *control* what you can and *negotiate* the rest. Can you relate to Tony? If technology has become an Energy Drain for you, determine what in particular is creating the biggest problem. Can you control your frustration by automating certain tasks or create a way to work around the system entirely? Can you delegate inputting or organizing information? Complicated systems often have several opponents who also have a deep knowledge of the design. See what they are doing to address problems or work around them. After you control what you can, determine how you are going to negotiate the rest.

Tips for Negotiating Technology Energy Drains

You may be on your own when negotiating technology. Here are things to try:

- **Take the time to learn the software you have.** Attend a class or ask your information technology (IT) people if you can work beside them. Go to the online tutorials. Many people don't use all the functions available because they don't understand them.

Stop Complainers and Energy Drainers

- **Accept that new technology takes time.** You will have to invest some amount of time to learn upgrades, new technologies, and different functionalities. You may also want to take a keyboarding course at a local community college to increase your speed and accuracy.

- **Start with small steps.** First, think about what technology gives you the most trouble and prioritize what you should do now. Start with one function that would dramatically help you. Then build on that knowledge.

- **Ask if others have found a solution or workaround.** Don't be afraid to ask questions, especially to the technology "natives." Create a network of people you can call upon to ask questions and share information. Don't forget to ask others for their best time-saving electronic tools.

 It's mindless interference in my work by people who don't have the capacity to complete their own.

Make a case to those in authority that the inefficiency, frustration, and morale issues cost the company in time wasted and reduced efficiency. Your arguments, especially if supported by others, may influence management to invest in the resources needed to eliminate the drama and allow employees to get more work done. However, if the technology fix is expensive and won't result in a significant increase in productivity, employees may gripe but still be forced to endure the inconvenience.

How to Negotiate Energy Drains Involving Bottlenecks

Energy Drains are situations where information or approval is delayed or "backed up." With Energy Drains, you have a lack of control or authority to get the input or direction you need. These are environments where the coworkers involved don't feel a sense of urgency which is compounded by a culture that lacks support, follow through, and communications.

Whatever may be the cause, stop beating your head against the wall or appealing to people who don't care. Instead, *identify, control, and manage the rest.*

 Coworkers who wait until the last minute to complete their portion cause undue stress on the other team players.

Jilted Judy

Judy couldn't believe it. She was still waiting on Anita and Rafi to turn over their estimates so that she could submit her proposal. Judy had requested the costs days ago. She couldn't wait any longer and still meet the deadline. Judy had e-mailed and texted them as well as leaving several messages on both on their office and cell phones. She had received one text back from Rafi that read "NP," which she guessed meant "No problem," but their lack of response *was* a problem. It was one more example of how the organization worked in "silos," with each department operating on its own. Judy went to their offices to see if she could find them. She was told by an assistant that they left early for a team happy hour. *"Well, I'm not happy,"* thought Judy.

On her way back, Judy stopped at her boss's office. Judy said, "Okay, Boss, tell me what I should do. Remember how I needed those figures from Anita and Rafi by close of business today? I haven't been able to reach Anita or Rafi by e-mail, text, or phone. What do you want to do? Do you want to send the proposal without the estimate? Do you want to call the client? What do you suggest?"

U-TURN First, *identify* the problem. Problems like this involve a bottleneck or interference, and you have no authority over others' responses. This lack of communication is also found internally when departments are "silos" or working independently and/or in isolation from each other.

Next, *control* what you can. In a case like this, question yourself: "Is this a real deadline? Could some information be left incomplete?" Then, *negotiate* the rest. In Judy's case, she asked her boss to decide how to meet the deadline and what steps to take next. The boss may also have some ideas on connecting with Anita and Rafi.

Consider engaging the help of your boss or a leader to advise you or, when necessary and appropriate, to negotiate on your behalf. Observe the actions of others who are successful breaking through the red tape, and follow their examples. See if you can determine mutual interests to gain others' commitment or find a solution that works around the bottleneck completely.

When Energy Drains increase, most people's capacity to handle challenges decreases, creating even more stress. Look for complaints about processes that do not work or red tape that is difficult to manage. Addressing the laundry list of Energy Drains can help address the problems you have with Complainers.

How to Negotiate Energy Drains of Too Much Work and Too Little Time

It's a problem we all suffer from: too much to do in a limited amount of time. You work late again, but the work keeps piling up and you never get caught up. You're not able to talk to people because you feel like you don't have time to breathe, think, or make decisions. You can't successfully handle the highest-priority projects because of emergencies and interruptions. You want to get work done, but other time wasters and emergencies are getting in the way.

These Energy Drains include excessive paperwork, over-scheduling, time management issues, technology challenges, interruptions, and lack of work-life balance. When trying to do everything at work, you end up missing everything at home, including family events, exercise, sleep, and simple relaxation. It is not healthy to suffer in silence. Instead, *identify, control, and negotiate the rest.*

Overworked William

As William left his third meeting of the day, his boss reminded him that the vendor search should take top priority. At least

15 voice-mail messages were from vendors wanting to know if they had made the final cut. Several vendors sent e-mails with amendments to their proposals. Today's small window of time to respond disappeared when William handled two escalations from stores.

William skipped lunch because two representatives dropped by to say "hi" when they were in the neighborhood. If he had time to catch up, he could put some systems in place to manage the work. For instance, he wanted to create a vendor Web page with proposal instructions, information regarding office visits, updates on decisions, and requests for information, and add both a dedicated e-mail and phone line.

William called his wife to vent:

"I don't know when I'll be home tonight. I had meetings all day, and they were a waste of time. Nobody was prepared, and nothing was accomplished. My inbox is overflowing, people keep interrupting me, and there are all these vendor proposals I haven't looked at yet. My voice-mail is maxed out, so who knows what calls I missed. Tell LeAnn I'm sorry that I'm going to have to miss her soccer game again. I'll make it up to her. I just need everyone around here to go home so I can think and get some of this work done."

U-TURN First, William needs to *identify the problem,* which is too much work and a lack of systems to support him. William needs to *control* what he can and *negotiate* the rest.

If you are in a similar situation, go to your boss and identify the different areas that stop you from doing your best job for the company. Propose eliminating some of the meetings, sending delegates, or updating the group in writing when things get

Energy Drains

busy. Get training on time management, delegation, and e-mail management. Create better systems for managing requests.

 My Energy Drain is people who can't wrap their minds around technology.

How to Negotiate Energy Drains Involving Misaligned Values

You feel hopeless and powerless. You're tolerating a hostile workplace that compromises your values. This situation can be more confusing if unethical actions of a boss or employees are tolerated, especially because of someone's ability to generate income. It is harder still if you need your paycheck and there aren't many options for other jobs available.

One of the most difficult office issues is misaligned values between you and your boss or organization. Misaligned values can involve harassment, lies, a hostile work environment, poor leadership, and a possible misuse of company funds. Most important, misaligned values result in you feeling as if you're being asked to go against your moral compass. Don't go against your own values. Instead, *identify, control, and negotiate the rest.*

 I lose at office politics every time.

Sam the Sleaze

Angela is a litigation assistant to Sam, one of the senior partners of a law firm. He is a rainmaker, and clients love him.

He is also a sleaze. With all the information about sexual harassment and discrimination, his actions are unbelievable. Up to this point, all the attorneys Angela has worked for are professional, hardworking, and respectful. Not Sam. He likes to try to shock her with jokes and sexual innuendos. From his expense reports, she knows Sam takes clients to gentlemen's clubs for "business development."

One associate told her privately that he was glad his wife didn't know what went on at the firm. The attorney told her that others had complained about Sam in the past but that "Sam pulls a lot of weight in this firm." Sam gives explicit instructions to clear his afternoon calendar on Tuesdays. If anyone calls, especially his wife, Angela is to say Sam is in a meeting and can't be interrupted. This "meeting" is held each Tuesday, two blocks away in a hotel, and it involves the associate with whom he is having an affair. Today is Tuesday, and the receptionist calls Angela.

"Angela, Sam's wife is holding on line two and asking to speak to you. She has an emergency with one of their kids. She can't reach him on his cell and wants to know why I can't get him out of the meeting. What do we do?"

Angela tells Sam's wife she'll try to reach him and leaves messages on his cell and at the hotel. Then, Angela decides it's time to stop enduring Sam's actions and telling lies on his behalf. She takes a deep breath and calls an employment attorney at her former firm for a consultation. With Sam's status as the firm rainmaker, his unwillingness to stop his behavior, and his apparent power over the firm's leadership, Angela wants professional advice *before* she takes her next step.

145

Energy Drains

U-TURN When you find yourself facing a harassing situation or working in an environment that doesn't align with your values, first *identify the problem* and what you can *control*. Often you can't control enough of the situation to change it. If you can *negotiate it,* try transferring internally, seeking another job, and approaching human resources (HR) or a champion in management for help.

Like Angela, sometimes no one can help you internally. In those cases, you might seek outside legal counsel. Knowledge gives you power. If you find out you have a claim, you can consider your next steps. If you receive advice that there is nothing illegal occurring or that you have a claim but it isn't worth the money to pursue it, you can make an informed decision. When you pay for advice, you have the choice to use all or part of it, ignore it entirely, or seek additional advice. Remember, you are in control. *You* are making determinations about what *you* want to do with *your* career.

If your Energy Drain is a harasser, turning to HR may be the wisest choice. Often, HR can support you in the best approach and intervene to stop the harassment.

How to Negotiate Energy Drains Involving Depressing Environments

Another Energy Drain is a depressing workplace environment filled with interruptions, distractions, technology challenges, noise, and a lack of privacy. Anyone is challenged in a work environment that doesn't support his or her work needs.

A poor working environment creates stress, depression, and lower productivity. Don't be a victim. You do not need to resign yourself to working in such an environment and taking no action. Instead, *identify, control, and negotiate the rest.*

Patti the Prisoner

The recent move to the new offices isn't popular, especially with Patti. Noises and loud voices bounce off the office space. Phones ring at empty desks because they aren't routed correctly or people forget to forward them when they leave their desks. The leaders have offices around the perimeter with windows and can shut their doors. Patti shares her cubicle with another coworker.

Patti told her friend at lunch:

"I'm so glad you could meet. I needed to escape our new offices. What a dump. I don't know how we're supposed to be innovative when everything around us looks more like the company's storage unit than a professional office. I sit in the middle of this maze of cubes that anyone over 4 feet tall can see over. There's no privacy. I heard all about one person's hospital visit yesterday, and today it was a discussion about fantasy football teams. I can't believe I have to share a cubicle. The man talks nonstop. Actually, it feels like a prison. I'm locked up in a cell with an inmate who won't shut up. It's miserable."

 Environmental problems aren't too difficult to *identify*. If your workplace environment isn't working, determine your options. What can you *control*? Can you negotiate flex time where you have the ability to adjust your work hours or to work from home several days a week? A solution to the cubicles is moving or seeing whether the partitions could be raised. See if you can get IT to do something about the ringing phones or physically go around and turn down the ringers of those at empty areas. To *negotiate* that work interruption, bring noise-cancelling headphones and listen to music when you don't need to be on the phone. Find an empty office or conference room to make calls. Personalize your space with décor, including a lamp with good lighting, plants, art, or personal items to help make your area feel more uplifting.

> I have found that having my ear buds in when I'm at my computer (the sound can be off, but the appearance is that I'm listening to music) has provided a much better personal environment to work in.

 Travel Tips to Stop Energy Drains

Here's what you need to know before you attempt to negotiate work drama caused by Energy Drains:

Reactions. Energy Drains are systems and situations that create stress, worry, anxiety, tension, loss of focus, exasperation, impatience, and confusion. They are time-consuming, oppressive, frustrating, demanding, and hectic. With Energy Drains, you feel uneasy, fearful, apprehensive, and troubled.

Reality. Energy Drains are environmental factors, organizational constraints, and systems and processes that place unnecessary stress on employees. They involve a lack of direction or unclear expectations. Energy Drains are caused by ill-suited work, political oversight, delays, mistakes, and office politics. They are cumbersome and involve poor communication, too much work, or a lack of work. Energy Drains include bottlenecks, a lack of systems, poor workflow management, inefficiencies, and policies and systems that don't make sense.

 It won't work to lose patience or become emotional, to ignore or postpone addressing them, or to fight the system or situation.

 The best way to negotiate with situations caused by Energy Drains is to *identify, control, and manage the rest.*

Identify. What is the problem? What will make the biggest difference? Who has input?

Control. Put a system in place that works. Create boundaries. Plan where you're able. Control what you can.

Negotiate the rest. Enforce a system. Remove yourself from unnecessary e-mails, calls, and meetings.

Chapter 8

How to Negotiate Work Drama

Prepare for Detours and Roadblocks

Spot Work Drama

Work drama is as inevitable as traffic jams. If you live and work with other people, you negotiate regularly with both traffic and drama. Wouldn't it be nice to be able to post warning signs around your *known* offenders? You could point out the Complainers and Energy Drains you've spotted and caution others to prepare for detours and roadblocks.

Classic Slogans about Complainers

Unfortunately, posting signs around the office isn't enough to deter chronic Complainers. Classics are:

"No Dumping"

"No Complaining Zone"

"If You're Not Part of the Solution, You're Part of the Problem"

"Lead, Follow, or Get Out of the Way"

"Put Up or Shut Up"

For more go to www.StopComplainers.com.

Are You Negotiating Work Drama?

Determining *where* you have work drama isn't difficult. Complainers and Energy Drains are obvious. Work drama:

- reduces productivity and innovation.
- creates a lack of trust and support among employees, peers, and leadership.
- results in unnecessary investments of time, energy, and money.
- produces confusion and a negative atmosphere.
- costs your organization high performers and devalues your reputation.
- distracts everyone from getting work done.

Reaction. Work drama creates stress, worry, loss of focus, poor performance, confusion, and turmoil. When faced with work drama, people are less likely to help each other, they struggle to find solutions, and have difficulties driving the organization's objectives.

Reality. Some work drama resolves itself over time. However, most challenges need attention or they won't go away. In a negotiation with anyone, you prepare by determining each party's interests, investments, risks, and potential rewards. That same preparation is necessary when you negotiate with Complainers or people who you want to support your efforts.

Stop Work Drama

Actions that Don't Work with Work Drama:

- **Hoping Complainers will change on their own.** Chronic Complainers aren't going to wake up one day and discard behavior that works for them. Without intervention, most won't decide to leave an organization that tolerates complaining. Reactively responding to problems as they occur is also a bad strategy.

- **Ignoring Energy Drains.** Environments and systems that don't function will not resolve on their own. Overlooking annoying situations, failing to address known stressors, and asking your high performers to be patient are easy ways to lose great people.

- **Not considering potential roadblocks or detours.** No matter how well you prepare, things go wrong. It's crazy not to think through potential problems or areas where you might go astray when you prepare to negotiate.

 The best way to negotiate work drama is to *decide to negotiate, find the right supporters, and plan for detours and roadblocks.*

- **Decide to negotiate.** Your first thought should be: *Is negotiating this work drama worth it to me?* To determine whether you want to engage in negotiations, ask yourself: What do I want? What are the solid business and personal reasons for supporting this change? Is this investment worth my time and effort? Is it worth the risk?

- **Find the right supporters.** Your thoughts regarding supporters should be: *Is negotiating work drama worth it to them?* Ask yourself: Who are the other stakeholders? Why is it in their best interests for others to support my efforts? When attempting to get support from people in authority positions, ask yourself: Is it likely I will have leadership's support? What do I want our leaders to do? What is realistic to expect from our organization?

- **Plan for detours and roadblocks.** When preparing, determine: *Where might I face additional challenges, and how can I anticipate them?* Ask: What could go wrong? What is my plan B? Have I left myself an out? Should I adjust course or proceed as planned? If I'm a leader, do I know how to best protect myself with questions, understanding policy, and documentation?

Decide to Negotiate

Instead of reacting to problems created by Complainers, take a proactive approach. This includes the choice of words you use when referring to Complainers. For instance, choose the proactive word *negotiate* instead of *handle, deal with,* or *manage.*

Negotiate is a stronger choice for several reasons. When you negotiate, you:

- establish yourself as being in the driver's seat.

- create a strategy to reach an agreement or resolve a disagreement.

- stay focused and on purpose.

- remain objective and logical, which helps you avoid the emotional potholes surrounding Complainers.

Work drama poses enough difficulties. It makes sense to use planning and techniques you already know. If you're in a business of any kind, you are familiar with negotiating to influence and reach positive outcomes. **Negotiation works.**

Decide to Avoid Hiring Complainers

- **Look for contributors.** Many Complainers wouldn't be employed if organizations placed as much weight on targeting candidates who make contributions to *culture* as well as making contributions to production.

- **Do your detective work.** Many poor performers are hired because companies fail to do the basics, such as checking references, background, experience, education, and skill sets.

- **Watch for actions that don't meet the "smell" test.** Ask questions about why someone wants to change teams or companies. Talk to others to get the full story. For example, some managers transfer their problem employees to other departments.

- **Use the interview process to spot potential Complainers or negative employees.** Your goal is to encourage applicants to talk and really *listen* to their

---

responses. Ask questions that provide insight into a person's character and working relationships such as:

- *How do you handle a coworker who will not do his/her fair share?*

- *Describe the best leader you ever had. How has that leader affected your leadership behavior?*

- *Tell me about a time when you failed and it wasn't your fault.*

You can download a list of insightful interview questions that seasoned HR professionals use in their selection process at www.StopComplainers.com.

Preparing to Negotiate Work Drama

Once you identify a problem with a Complainer, prepare to negotiate as you would any business opportunity. In this case, your objective is to stop the work drama. A second objective is that you'd like your Complainer to transform into a positive contributor if possible. To create your strategy, ask yourself these questions:

- **What do I want?** When you are clear on the destination or outcome you want, you improve your odds of reaching it. Describe how the environment would look, sound, and feel if the work drama stopped.

- **Why?** List the good business and personal reasons supporting this change. Business reasons that help you advocate change can include various costs such as amount of time, impact on productivity and morale, retention of coworkers, and disengagement. Your *personal* reasons are just as important and keep you motivated. Don't discount reasons such as, "I will be able to ask for the help I need," and "I will look forward to coming to work."

- **Is this investment worth my time and effort?** Decide if negotiating the drama is an investment you're willing to make. Determine whether there is a possibility that the issue could be resolved on its own. For instance, if your Complainer is new to the team, ask yourself: Is he or she here to stay, or has this person been brought in temporarily to address a specific problem or to perform unpopular tasks? For example, a manager may be brought in to bring an underperforming team into compliance. After the budgeting cuts, spending policy changes, reorganization, and/or layoffs have occurred, that manager is off to another assignment to make equally unpopular decisions with another team.

If you're a leader who is preparing to negotiate, also ask:

- **How will the environment change for the better if I address the Complainer's behavior?** A clear picture of an environment that includes well-adjusted employees who communicate well and work together to accomplish the most important business objectives is a motivating goal. Remind yourself of the positive outcomes of having a workforce of contributors so that you can stay engaged throughout the process.

- **Have I done everything I can to resolve the Energy Drains that create complaining?** If you fix Energy Drains by increasing communication, direction, and feedback or by improving technology, workflow, the environment, and the culture, you will see a decrease in complaints. Often, complaining goes away when the stressors are addressed or if you provide feedback to your Complainer.

 He thanked me for telling him what he was doing and how it was affecting others. He had never realized the impact of his complaining. Now, he is on a new path.

Find the Right Supporters

If you have decided to negotiate the work drama, identifying people who will support your actions and serve as your advocates is the next step. Find someone who believes you and is willing to take action. When people have a good impression of or a long-term relationship with a Complainer, it is more challenging to convince them that the negative behavior exists.

Making a Case for Leadership to Stop the Complainer

Approaching management for help with Complainers is often the best move. A company's leadership can provide insight, direction, and the history of employees with multiple problems. When you take your case against Complainers to the top, come prepared. Treat your request like a high-stakes negotiation where your reputation, performance, and job may come under scrutiny as well.

People in leadership are more likely to commit time and resources to resolve the work drama caused by a Complainer when you do the following:

- **Show it's in the company's best interest to act.** Point out good business reasons for the company's involvement. Determine the costs of time wasted and the effect on morale. Raise concerns regarding retention of coworkers, disengagement, and potential legal claims. Stating that a Complainer "has a bad attitude and I want him/her gone" isn't enough.

- **Prepare support.** You want to be able to discuss specific examples of how your Complainer negatively affects the organization before approaching leadership, human resources (HR), and owners for guidance or intervention.

In the Introduction, you are provided statistics, expert opinion, and other support to stop Complainers. Use that information as a starting point. Go to the Complainer Cost Calculator at www.StopComplainers.com, insert your number of employees, and determine what Complainers and Energy Drains cost your company.

- **Provide a clear description of the problems created by the Complainer.** Share the history, details, and which people are affected by the Complainer's behavior. Leaders want to know if the behavior violates company policy, procedure, or the law and/or exposes the company to risk.

- **Show how you or others have tried to stop the Complainer.** Address your issues before you involve management, complicate matters, and risk ruining relationships. Document your attempts. Show what has worked and what hasn't.

- **Define what you want the organization to do.** Determine whether you want advice, intervention, or permission.

- **Ask whether there is anything else you should know.** Perhaps corrective action is already in the works. There could be a potential lawsuit, governmental claim, or business reason to avoid action. Maybe others tried to correct the behavior and weren't effective. Learn what you can before acting.

U-TURN *Steps to Negotiate a Legal U-Turn*

If you're a leader, don't be surprised if your name appears on a legal complaint filed by an employee. To protect yourself and your company, follow some basic guidelines when you attempt to turn around a Complainer's behavior:

- **Be aware.** In the beginning, take the time to identify the situation, people involved, and possible causes.

- **Ask questions.** Listen and understand the real problem before you determine how you are going to act. Ask for history on the employee and what, if any, actions have been taken.

- **Make a decision.** Review your organization's policies and rules, involve HR and your boss, and then make an objective decision on the right direction.

- **Invest resources.** Allocate the proper time, energy, and attention to solve the problem.

- **Plan for jams, roadblocks, and detours.** Identify potential problems and the strategies you'll use when you face them.

- **Adjust course.** Revise your plan as needed and keep HR and your leader informed.

- **Evaluate progress.** Review your direction as needed with HR and your boss.

- **Document.** At a minimum, you'll be asked for your account of what happened. Record the Complainer's actions, the impact on the company, and document the steps you took to turn the situation around.

Turn to Human Resources for Help

When dealing with an experienced HR professional, you have someone who knows not only the law but how it blends when running an organization. If your HR team is respected in your organization and has a history of success, turn to them to help you with:

- communication techniques.
- ideas to manage different types of personalities.
- organizational strategy.
- identification of harassment or illegal activities.
- past actions of this employee.
- approaches tried with other employees including referrals to an EAP (Employee Assistance Program).

HR professionals will tell you there is a wide range of abilities in people who work in their field. Most HR professionals are excellent with great experience and training, but some have simply been handed the HR role with no training or help.

Turn the Problem Around Yourself

As with other professions, even in HR, there are differences in the individual professional's ability to manage employee issues. In different companies, there are also great variances in whether HR functions on behalf of the employees, the employer, or sometimes both. You will need to recognize whether your HR department could be helpful or a waste of time.

When surveyed, 11 percent of participants had left their jobs because of a Complainer. When asked to comment if they "told someone in authority about the Complainer and what action, if any, was taken," people replied:

- **No, I didn't tell.** One-third of the people did not ask for help or bring the Complainer to the company's attention before they left. Their reasons included, "It wasn't worth the trouble," "The Complainer was [my boss or owner or spouse/significant other of my boss or owner]," "Nobody cared," and "I took the chicken's way out and just quit."

- **Yes, I told.** The other 66 percent responded that they asked for help. Only one person said that things improved after coming forward. The others reported that telling someone in management and/or HR didn't work and, in several instances, made the problem worse. Employees reported that after speaking to HR, "Nothing was done," "I was told to have patience," "It took them too long to resolve," "It didn't work," "It was advised that I leave," "The Complainer was promoted," "Several of us did tell and then eventually left. The Complainer is still there," and "The company retaliated against me."

 I was told to love them through it and that it was just part of working on a team.

When Management Doesn't Help

Depending on the culture of an organization, a leadership team may do little to address the Complainer's negative behavior or an energy-draining problem. Unless it improves the bottom line or there is a good business reason to resolve it, some companies won't act. If leadership isn't willing to stop the Complainer, try to determine the reasons behind that unwillingness to act *before* moving ahead.

How to Negotiate Detours and Roadblocks

Like negotiating traffic jams, negotiating with Complainers is frustrating—plan on facing detours and roadblocks. As in traffic, a U-turn isn't always the safest or best solution. Instead, you can choose to proceed with the course you're on and leave the drama as it is, you can turn for direction and support from others, or you can choose to exit the situation altogether.

Plan for Detours

Many people worry and even fixate about the potential hazards and the things that can go wrong. Successful negotiators pinpoint their potential problems, know their alternatives, and create a strategy *before* they begin. Here are some tips to help you prepare:

- **Know what could go wrong.** The Complainer could create problems. What are those potential problems? Who or what else could create problems for you?
- **Identify your worst-case scenario.** If your worst-case scenario involves your Complainer becoming irritated and gossiping about you to another coworker,

you don't have much to lose. However, if your worst-case scenario includes you being reprimanded, fired, or shut out of decisions and the chances of finding another job right now are slim, rethink your strategy.

What Can Go Wrong?

- List everything you can think of that could go wrong.

- Identify your worst-case scenario and theirs; write them down.

- Assign a percentage that the worst-case scenarios will occur.

- Ask, "Can I live with the risk?" and "Can they live with their risk?"

- Taking into account what can go wrong in your worst-case scenario, ask, "Can I live with myself if I do not try to turn the situation around?"

Things go wrong in any negotiation. If you can't live with your worst-case scenario, you don't have the right plan.

- **Know your plan B.** Prepare your next step(s) if the approach with the Complainer doesn't work. Identify someone you could ask for help. Know what actions or reactions would trigger a different route or even an exit.

Plan for Roadblocks

Most negotiations, especially with Complainers, aren't executed flawlessly. It's easy to second-guess your decisions and lose confidence when things aren't going as planned. Ask yourself questions *before* you begin. Later, if things aren't working the way you anticipated and you're in the middle of a messy negotiation, you won't question your initial decision to act. When you feel your plans are not progressing or that negotiating the work drama isn't working, consider the following:

- **Give the plan time to work.** Make sure you've allowed enough time for the change to occur. Don't second-guess yourself because you feel uncomfortable or the situation gets messy *until* you have gained additional insight or determined you're on the wrong course.

- **Leave yourself an out.** Driver's education students are told to "leave yourself an out" or a lane to move into in case of an emergency. Don't be forced to act if it isn't the right timing. Give yourself permission to take a break to think, especially if you're in a heated situation or dealing with a disgruntled employee. Schedule a follow-up meeting or ask if you can call the Complainer back later.

- **Determine the real reasons you are questioning your decision to act.** Before you adjust your course, determine the real reasons you are questioning your decisions. It may seem you are investing too much effort or time and that the Complainer isn't changing fast enough. Before you change your strategy, ask yourself these questions:

- Have you gained additional information or insight that makes this direction less desirable?

- Are you feeling uncomfortable because you're trying something new?

 Travel Tips to Negotiate Work Drama

Negotiating work drama is as inconvenient and frustrating as negotiating traffic. Here's what you need to know before you attempt to negotiate work drama:

Reactions. Work drama creates stress, worry, loss of focus, poor performance, confusion, and turmoil. When faced with work drama, people are less likely to trust, help each other, find solutions, or drive the success of an organization.

Reality. Some work drama resolves itself with time. Identifying those temporary situations is important. However, waiting too long or reactively responding to problems as they occur creates additional issues. Failing to address a chronic Complainer's behavior or a known Energy Drain causes a reduction of productivity, a lack of trust, a negative atmosphere, and may cost you good performers.

 Actions that don't work are hoping Complainers will change on their own, ignoring Energy Drains, or asking your high performers to be patient.

Stop Complainers and Energy Drainers

U-TURN The best way to negotiate work drama is to *decide to negotiate, find the right supporters, and plan for detours and roadblocks.*

Decide to negotiate. Your first decision should be: *Is negotiating work drama worth it to me?* To determine if you want to engage, ask yourself: What do I want? What are the solid business and personal reasons for supporting this change? Is this investment worth my time and effort? Is it worth the risk?

Find the right supporters. With regard to supporters, determine: *Is negotiating work drama worth it to them?* Ask yourself: Who are the other stakeholders? Why is it in their best interest for others to support my efforts? When attempting to get support from people in authority positions, ask yourself: Is it likely I will have leadership's support? What do I want our leaders to do? What do I want the organization to do?

Plan for detours and roadblocks. When preparing, determine: *Where might I face additional challenges, and how can I anticipate them?* Ask: What could go wrong? What is my plan B? Have I left myself an out? Should I adjust course or proceed as planned? If I'm a leader, do I know how to best protect myself with questions, understanding policy, and documentation?

Chapter 9

Go Ahead, Complain

Proceed with Care

When you think of *constructive* complaining, you think, "Please proceed. Right this way." In business, you need all the insight and help you can get to improve. In many cases, people who are brave enough to speak up are voicing the experience of several. When faced with complaining, it is best to follow these guidelines: *Listen to complaints. Encourage constructive feedback. Complain effectively and offer solutions.*

Spot Complaints

Not all complaining by employees is bad. People often have legitimate complaints that deserve attention, such as too much work or poor workflow management. Pay special attention to complaints involving potential harm to individuals, unethical behavior, or illegal actions. Legitimate complaints include:

- unclear direction or lack of feedback from leaders.
- bullying, harassment, or unsafe working conditions.
- job fear and/or undue pressure to perform.
- information about someone lying, cheating, or breaking the law.
- unrealistic demands from clients or customers.
- incompetent coworkers or peers not pulling their weight or holding others up.
- not feeling heard or respected at work.

Part of any job is to figure out how to work with other people and get the best you can from them. This is a fact of business.

Employee Complaints Are Good

The consequences for companies that don't listen to their people are common. Employees find a way to be heard through lawsuits, strikes, slow-downs, and whistleblowing. Some leaders encourage their employees to provide feedback and concerns. These leaders recognize the positive power of input, complaints, and venting.

Former Southwest Airlines chief executive officer (CEO) Howard Putnam's solution to increase employee morale and communications at another airline, Braniff, was to send a personal letter to the airline's 10,000 employees and families at their homes. Putnam asked discouraged employees to give suggestions to improve the company's revenue, cut costs, and add to the quality of operations. Putnam received more than 3,000 responses, suggestions, and complaints, which ranged from an employee's missed check to the existence of an inside ring of thieves.

"CEOs who take listening seriously, and I did, know the value of input from all stakeholders, especially employees on the front line. There is valuable knowledge available . . . at no charge out there . . . take advantage of it and utilize it." Putnam acknowledged the feedback, too. Each employee who wrote him received a handwritten note from

Putnam in which he thanked them for writing and commented on their suggestions. Putnam says, "They never had a handwritten note from the CEO before. They saved the notes. They shared them with customers and the media. The improved morale was instantaneous, and customer service and satisfaction went up immediately as well. The value of a handwritten note, still today in this electronic age, is amazing."

Encourage Employees to Give Valid Complaints and Solutions

Create an environment where people are encouraged to share their ideas and feel empowered to make changes. Employees who feel they are being heard *and* have the ability to create changes are less likely to complain.

Address Complaints and Investigate Their Validity

Establish a formal complaint process. By having a complaint system in place, people are more likely to think through their complaint and offer solutions. And providing a structured outlet may keep them from complaining to others. Those who are just whining are less likely to spend time filing a formal complaint.

Maintain a positive attitude in general. Bosses and coworkers who make a conscious effort to control their moods and stay upbeat positively influence a group. A boss or coworker who complains is more likely to have employees who complain as well.

My Complainer stopped complaining when I treated her with respect and got her opinion on improving work productivity in certain office concerns. She left feeling valued and a team player.

Stop Complainers at Work by Listening to Them

Consider your Complainers at work. They may be providing helpful information, but just not presenting it well. Review the feedback they give and look for nuggets of truth. In some cases, your Complainers may be an early warning system and a more vocal representation of your own workforce. Step back and think about their complaints in a broader context. For instance:

- **Whiners** want to receive *empathy* and *connect*. Their behavior may signal to you that you or other leaders are not communicating effectively, that a work-life balance issue exists, or that work has been unevenly dispersed among the team.

- **Complicators** are seeking *calm* and *stability*. Their behavior may signal that there has been too much change or too little communication or that something is about to break if it is not addressed.

- **Prima Donnas** are seeking *recognition*. Their poor behavior may be an indication that others need more support and recognition for the jobs they are doing.

- **Controllers** want *action*. They are looking to get things done. Their behavior may show you that something or

175

Go Ahead, Complain

someone is blocking their progress and the progress of others.

- **Toxics** are trying to *create unhealthy situations.* They get an almost sadistic enjoyment out of manipulating others. The more they act up, the more others may need relief.

In all of these situations, don't forget to solicit solutions from the people bringing the complaints. Use phrases such as, "Sounds like a problem. What are you going to do?" and "What do you think would be the best solution to this?"

Complaining Is Good for Business

It sounds unbelievable, but criticism can create beneficial business results. Complainers who take the time and energy to identify an area of concern are doing you a favor. A client who points out a glitch in fulfillment or a service delivery issue might actually be helping you retain other clients. If situations are brought to light early enough, a company has the opportunity to make it right. It's common knowledge that people who have problems that are resolved correctly are more loyal to the company and even refer more business.

 When the customer saw that we were taking him seriously, the complaints reduced significantly. Not entirely, mind you, because he seemed to rather enjoy complaining about some things.

Tips to Encourage Constructive Feedback

Listen to the Complainer without judgment.

Don't try to explain your point of view.

Use phrases such as, "I wish we could have met under different circumstances."

Don't blame.

Show appreciation for the information. "Thank you for bringing that to my attention."

Highlight mutual interests. "It sounds like this isn't working. Neither of us wants that."

Show empathy but monitor "yes" and "you're right" responses. The Complainer may not be correct.

Do not dwell on past. Spend 90 percent of the conversation focusing on the future. "Let's build on what we have done right and get this issue resolved."

Understand your audience and focus on stakeholders. What are their interests here?

If you are in the wrong, say, "What can we do to make it right?" or "What do you think is fair?"

Use phrases such as, "Taking all that into consideration, I can see why you feel that way."

Know the appropriate time to get help from a superior.

When in doubt, ask questions.

A vendor who identifies areas of concern, such as payment processing issues, helps the company ensure that contracts are fulfilled. An employee who gripes about a frustrating policy gives you an opportunity to remove an obstacle that may be affecting other employees. Do your best not to disregard the complaint because you dislike the way it's presented to you. If the Complainer isn't professional, does not communicate effectively, or uses inappropriate language, do not automatically dismiss the message. If the complaint is valid, address the problem.

Former *Fort Worth Star-Telegram* columnist and author Dave Lieber provides a popular forum that allows individuals to protest and take action. "Smart companies use complaints to fix their problems," Lieber says. "The complaints are not only empowering for the customers but also for the companies that want to build strong relationships and maintain their reputations."

Business leaders who are responsive and handle complaints effectively often gain a more loyal community. In your attempt to understand the situation, show empathy for the Complainer. The actions you take to remedy the problem could save you an important customer, valued partner, or critical employee!

A Client's Destructive Feedback

Clients who don't want their problems resolved may simply want an avenue to vent. At times, clients and customers take advantage of service providers. Clients can seek people like customer service representatives who are paid to listen to them. The client Complainer then spews issues and emotions caused by some ill fortune or personal baggage. These chronic complaining customers "show up" and verbally "throw up" all over you and your people. Approximately 27 percent of people surveyed said that customers and clients were their Complainers.

As a leader, give your direct reports words/phrases they can say to decrease the hostility. Let them know when they need to escalate the issue up the leadership chain. Remind your people that, in the process of hearing the complaints, they are receiving valuable feedback that assists the company in fixing problems. Help your employees manage these sometimes difficult customer relationships. Give the customer service representatives permission to take a break, postpone a decision until they know the right action, and even fire a client if the situation requires it. Remember, you and your people are not punching bags.

 Communication is key: from work to relationships to life in general. If you don't communicate, the problem is yours, not theirs.

Complaining Is Good for You

Complaining can be personally beneficial. If you receive poor service, complaining gives the service provider an opportunity to make it right for you. Complaining gives you an opportunity to vent and determine the validity of your feelings. Complaining allows you to connect with others. Other people may have similar complaints. Until one person voices his or her concerns, others may not speak up.

Complaining is personally beneficial when it:

- allows you to determine whether others share your frustration or concern.

- permits you to vent, which can be cathartic, versus keeping it in and putting up with stress.

- shows dissatisfaction in a more permissible way than bad actions.

- enables you to effectively be heard or have your needs met (for example, a squeaky wheel is heard and often fixed).

- serves as an icebreaker when meeting new people (for example, "The line here always takes too long," or "Can you believe how terribly the Dallas Cowboys played on Sunday?").

- helps you save face in front of others to provide an excuse for your behavior (for example, "I would've done better on the team presentation if my headache wasn't so bad," or "I couldn't run as fast in the 5K because my ankle is sore").

- prevents you from ruminating about discontent so that it doesn't fester and blow up into something bigger than it is and cause depression.[1]

"People don't realize how much power they have to fix situations, often quickly and in their favor," Lieber says. His

"Watchdog" newspaper column, book, and programs help empower others to complain effectively and protect themselves from unethical individuals and companies.

"If something goes wrong, speak up. You can get what others can't. . . . Most people don't realize how easy this is."

Making a Valid Complaint

If you want to be more effective when you are lodging a valid complaint, make sure to use the negotiation questions:

- What do I want from my complaint?
- What good business reasons support my request?
- Is it worth my time and effort?
- What good business reasons does the other side have to address my complaint?
- What shared interests, if any, do we have?

 Travel Tips to Complain Constructively

Here's what you need to know before you listen to complaints, encourage feedback, or attempt to complain effectively:

 Reactions. Employees and customers have *legitimate* complaints that deserve attention.
(continued)

(*continued*)

Complaints can point out problems or issues that need to be corrected at your business. Complaining is good for your health because it keeps you from holding in potential stress.

Reality. In business, you welcome *constructive* complaining and the insight it brings to help you improve. In many cases, people who are brave enough to speak up are voicing the experience of several. Listen to those complaints. Give people with real complaints the ability to tell them to the company first, not an outsider. Have a productive way to capture constructive feedback and correct issues.

 If you are working with or leading Complainers, remember that you won't stop their complaining. You just want them to stop complaining to you.

U-TURN The best way to negotiate complaining is to *listen to complaints, encourage constructive feedback, complain effectively, and offer solutions.* And, if you're the Complainer, don't complain all the time. You are giving your power away to those who express themselves more effectively. If you have a problem and want help, it's your responsibility to identify what you need, calmly approach others, and bring some solutions. Remember, you want to communicate powerfully so that others will listen and help you get what you want.

Winning Beats Whining

You're almost finished. Do you have any complaints? Did this book deliver as promised? Do you now have tools to identify Complainers? Were you provided with examples, suggestions, scenarios, conversation strategies, and ideas to negotiate to get support from your company? Can you identify those Energy Drains that are creating stress? Have you created a plan of action? Have you browsed the Resources? What about the website links? If you are a Complainer, do you have some ideas of what to do next? If you didn't receive something you needed, let us know at www.StopComplainers.com.

And if you did receive what was promised, what are you waiting for? Make the decision to negotiate your work drama and get help if needed. *If you have Energy Drains*, identify them and correct them if possible. Do what you can to alleviate the unnecessary stress so that everyone can get back to work and get more done. *If you are seen as a Complainer,* you can *stop* it. Seek help if you need it. Complaining isn't reflective of who you really are or the gifts and talents you can contribute. Develop your strengths and learn how to communicate so that others will help you get what you want.

And if you have chronic Complainers, give them feedback, redirect their focus, influence them positively, and see if they will choose to be contributors. You no longer have to manage, deal with, or tolerate chronic complaining. You now have the strategy, tools, and support to negotiate that unnecessary and expensive work drama. And with those Complainers and Energy Drains, you now have the power and permission to *spot them and stop them.*

Help Ahead

Complain-a-Grams to Complainer or Company Leader

If you want an *anonymous* way to notify someone that he or she is a Complainer or notify someone in leadership that there are Complainers or Energy Drains, you can copy these letters or download Complain-a-Grams from www.StopComplainers .com. Simply place a Complain-a-Gram with a copy of this book on the Complainer's or leader's desk when no one is around, or mail the note and book in an envelope addressed to him or her . . . without a return address of course!

COMPLAIN-A-GRAM

Hello.

You are receiving this note and book because you may have a tendency to complain when the going gets tough. Someone cares about you and wants to make sure that you aren't seen that way by others. This perception may or may not be real. From time to time, all of us use complaining behavior when we're under stress. To see if complaining may be an issue for you, please take the free assessment "Are You Seen as a Complainer?" at www.StopComplainers .com. The results are confidential and provided to you as a resource for your own personal development.

If you find you have traits that no longer serve you, please read Chapters 6–9 to find out what type of complaining you may be doing, ways to eliminate situations that might be causing you to complain, and ideas to positively raise issues and get the results you want.

Someone cares enough about you—and your success— to pay for you to have this material and has taken the time to give it to you. That's an investment in your future. *Please read it.*

Disclaimer: Sending you this book is not an action endorsed by your company, organization, the author or the publisher. In purchasing this book and in taking the free assessment provided, no information about your identity, your company or your performance is collected, unless you want your results sent to you by e-mail. This Complain-a-Gram is one person's opinion and may or may not be accurate.

COMPLAIN-A-GRAM

Hello.

You are receiving this book because someone believes you have Complainers and Energy Drains in your workplace. Someone who cares about this company—and its success—wants to make sure that you maintain high performance, retain your top performers, and continue your fine business reputation.

To see if complaining may be an issue for your organization, please take the free assessment "Spot Your Complainer's Type" at www.StopComplainers.com.

Complainers are expensive. According to a survey of more than 1,000 participants, 78 percent of people are spending at least 3 to 6 hours a week wasting their time dealing with Complainers rather than focusing on "real work" that produces results! **To calculate your potential Complainer cost per year, go to www.StopComplainers.com.**

Someone purchased these materials and gave them to you as a leader because they believe you care enough about your business to make the changes required to improve the team, workplace, and performance. That's an investment in your organization's future. *Please read it.*

Disclaimer: Sending you this book is not an action endorsed by your company, organization, the author or the publisher. In purchasing this book and in taking the free assessment provided, no information about your identity, your company or your performance is collected, unless you want your results sent to you by e-mail. This Complain-a-Gram is one person's opinion and may or may not be accurate.

Complainer Type Road Signs and Slogans

In the Complain-a-Grams, recipients are asked to go to www.StopComplainers.com and take the "Spot Your Complainer's Type" or "Am I Seen as a Complainer?" The results of the assessments identify the type of Complainer, the frequency of complaining, a comparison to others' results, and strategies to *stop* the behavior you *spot*.

Each Complainer type has its own road sign and slogan. These help you remember the wants of the Complainer and which strategies work when negotiating with your particular Complainer type.

Whiners

Help Me Across

Complicators

Slow Uphill Climb

Prima Donnas

Pay Attention

Controllers

Yield to Me

Toxics

Hazardous to Your Health

Conversation Strategies per Complainer Type

It came as a surprise when the survey results revealed *five* different types of Complainers. Each of the five types has a specific way of complaining, including tone, conversation style, words, and behavior. The five types of Complainers also want different outcomes: empathy, stability, attention, results, and control. Here are strategies to turn Complainers to contributors.

- **Whiners** want empathy and connection. They complain by showing disapproval, venting, or withdrawing.

    The best way to negotiate is to listen, empathize, and ask for solutions. Remind Whiners that people want to connect more with problem solvers, not just problem suppliers.

    Gain leadership's support by spotting decisions not made and work not accomplished due to behavior.

- **Complicators** want calm and stability. They complain by blocking, complicating, and creating confusion.

    The best way to negotiate is to reduce speed, respect effort, and upgrade. Remind Complicators that change is inevitable. They can upgrade systems or not have input.

    Gain leadership's support by spotting unnecessary complications, delays, and blocks created by behavior.

- **Prima Donnas** want recognition. They complain by seeking attention, gossiping, interrupting, and interfering.

The best way to negotiate is to acknowledge, avoid getting lost in the drama, and publicize. Remind Prima Donnas that positive recognition beats a bad reputation.

Gain leadership's support by spotting results created by disruption, low accountability, gossip, and distraction.

- **Controllers** want action and to accomplish goals. They complain aggressively to control or reach an outcome.

  The best way to negotiate is to stand, deliver, and let them decide. Remind Controllers that to achieve lasting results, you need willing performers, not coerced victims.

  Gain leadership's support by spotting risks of bullying, intimidating, harassing, and demeaning behavior.

- **Toxics** want to further a self-absorbed agenda. They complain to manipulate and poison the environment.

  The best way to negotiate is to protect yourself, watch, and steer clear. Remind Toxics that improving sensitivity and building trust will help them achieve their individual goals.

  Gain leadership's support by spotting turmoil, new problems, and manipulation of others by poisoning behavior.

Related Communication Styles

In general, Complainer types correlate with commonly recognized styles of communication. The Complainers represent the dark side or negative behaviors that appear when people are placed under stress. Please see the following table for general descriptions identifying each type of Complainer and behaviors under stress as well as areas for improvement and development. Also listed are popular profiles and assessments that identify communication styles. Although these profiles don't map precisely to each Complainer type, they each offer extensive coaching and training tools to help you and your Complainer identify strengths and communication strategies.

Complainer Types	Neutral Traits	Development Opportunities	Related Communication Styles
Whiners			
Under stress: Passive, submissive, withdrawn, silent, tearful, sensitive, hurt	Introverted Reserved Casual Sensing Feelers Relationship-oriented	*Improve coping skills through:* Assertiveness, self-care, independent decision making *Enhance natural strengths in:* Mediation, team building, conflict resolution, listening	Phlegmatic/Hippocrates Relater/CORE MAP ISF/Myers-Briggs Sensors/Supportiveness/DiSC Conciliator/BrainStyles Blue/Personal Insight Inventory
Under extreme stress: Explode			
Complicators			
Under stress: Passive-aggressive, narrow-minded, cold, withdrawn, critical, resistant, stubborn	Introverted Reserved Serious Sensing Thinkers Task-oriented	*Improve coping skills through:* Relaxation, flexibility, letting go of perfectionism, emotional intelligence *Enhance natural strengths in:* Planning, strategy, project management, organization	Melancholy/Hippocrates Organizer/CORE MAP IST/Myers-Briggs Compliance/ Conscientiousness/DiSC Deliberator/BrainStyles Green/Personal Insight Inventory
Under extreme stress: Explode			

Stop Complainers and Energy Drainers

Complainer Types	Neutral Traits	Development Opportunities	Related Communication Styles
Prima Donnas			
Under stress: Aggressive, pushy, loud, argumentative, disruptive, impatient	Extroverted Bold Casual Intuitive	*Improve coping skills through:* Impulse control, planning, internal validation	Sanguine/Hippocrates Entertainer/CORE MAP ENF/Myers-Briggs Inducement/Influence/DiSC
Under extreme stress: Shut down	Feeling Relationship-oriented	*Enhance natural strengths in:* Networking, public speaking, multitasking, creativity	Conceptor/BrainStyles Yellow/Personal Insight Inventory
Controllers			
Under stress: Aggressive, bossy, loud, demanding, impatient, bully	Extroverted Assertive Serious Intuitive	*Improve coping skills through:* Communication, patience, sensitivity, trusting others	Choleric/Hippocrates Commander/CORE MAP ENT/Myers-Briggs Director/Dominance/DiSC
Under extreme stress: Shut down	Thinkers Task-oriented	*Enhance natural strengths in:* Negotiations, influence, risk taking, decisions	Knower/BrainStyles Red/Personal Insight Inventory

Note: Any type can be a Toxic personality. In all instances they have been conditioned away from their natural style and toward passive-aggressive behavior. In the extreme these are the sociopaths and psychopaths.

Negotiating Work Drama Checklists

Determine Direction to Take

Questions and Decisions	Strategy
Work Drama Description *Complainer Type? Traits to Consider?* ☐ Whiner ☐ Complicator ☐ Prima Donna ☐ Controller ☐ Toxic ☐ Combination *Determine types at www.StopComplainers.com* *Who? (Name, role, history, status)* *How is he or she perceived by others?* Or *Energy Drain Type? Items to Consider?* ☐ Direction/lack of leadership ☐ Bottlenecks/red tape ☐ Technology challenges ☐ Paperwork/overscheduling ☐ Interruptions/multiple meetings ☐ Environment/cultural issues *Who is affected? How? Frequency?*	
Impact *How does behavior or situation negatively impact business or others?*	
Best Direction to Take *At this time, I'm choosing to:* ☐ Proceed with Current Approach and/or Wait ☐ Turn to Others (Who? & for What?) ☐ Exit (Transfer or Change Jobs) ☐ Negotiate to Turn Drama Around	

Stop Complainers and Energy Drainers

Prepare to Negotiate Work Drama

Questions and Decisions	Strategy
Decide to Negotiate *What do I want?* What are *my* personal reasons? How will the environment be better? *Is it worth investing my time and effort?* Does a potential reward outweigh my risk?	
Find the Right Supporters *Who are the other stakeholders?* How do others perceive my Complainer? Why is a change in their best interests? *What do I want our leaders to do?* What supporting documentation exists? What is *realistic* to expect from our organization?	
Detours and Roadblocks *What could go wrong?* What is my worst-case scenario? Can I live with it? *What is my alternative or plan B?* Have I left myself an out? Should I adjust course or proceed as planned?	

Remember, *you* are in the driver's seat of *your* life and *your* career. Whether *you* decide to negotiate or not is *your* decision! Even if you determine to pursue another direction, the exercise of preparing a plan of action allows you to: think logically about work drama; create a roadmap if you later decide to turn things around; and attempt portions of negotiating now.

Negotiate Your Work Drama

Questions and Decisions	Strategy
Set the Scene ***Where will I have this conversation?*** (ex. A private place without distraction.) ***How will I start the conversation?*** (ex. "I'm afraid I have difficult news." Or "I've observed a serious issue.")	
Negotiate with a Complainer ***Will a leader representative be present?*** *If so*, what is our plan and what role does he or she play? *If not*, have I warned leadership about possible reaction? ***What Complainer type do I have and*** ***what traits do I need to keep in mind?*** What will I say if my Complainer vents or becomes emotional?	
Negotiate to Stop Energy Drain ***What Energy Drain type do I have?*** How is investing expense and effort to correct drama a good business decision?	
Conversation ***What objections do I anticipate and*** ***how will I respond?*** What is my "out" or escape if needed? (ex. "I need to take a break.")	
Wrap Up ***What is our agreement or next step?*** How will I document?	

Additional questions for determining your strategy in negotiating work drama are available at www.StopComplainers.com under Tools and Resources.

Stop Complainers and Energy Drainers

Notes

Work Drama 101

1. In the survey, 45.4 percent of the respondents reported that Complainers and draining situations take up 3 to 6 hours of their workweek, and another 31.7 percent reported that they take up more than 6 hours per week. Within these totals, 2.1 percent actually reported that Complainers and Energy Drains consume more than 20 hours of their time during their workweek. *In other words, over 77 percent (45.4% + 31.7% =77.1%) of the survey respondents reported a minimum of 3 to 6 hours per week being wasted.*

   According to the US Department of Labor Bureau of Labor Statistics' report "Employer Costs for Employee Compensation—June 2012," the average cost for a private industry company worker is $28.80 per hour; for state and local government workers, $41.10 per hour; for service workers, $14.01 per hour; and for management and professional workers, $51.23 per hour (benefits are approximately 30 percent of these costs).

   The US Worker calculation was derived from using $28.20 (the lowest average hourly wage of US workers) *multiplied* by three hours a week (the lowest amount of hours reported wasted by 77% of survey participants) *multiplied* by 77% of 155,696,000 (US employed workers according to the US Department of Labor Bureau of Statistics on November 2, 2012) *for a total of*

$10,142,348,832 wasted time per week and multiplied by 50 work-weeks in a year is $507,117,600 of wasted time per year. www.Stop Complainers.com/survey; http://www.bls.gov/opub/ted/2012/ted_20120919.htm; and http://www.bls.gov/news.release/archives/ecec_09112012.pdf.

2. "How to Fire People the Right Way" by Meridith Levinson, CIO.com, http://www.cio.com/article/692778/How_to_Fire_People_the_Right_Way?page=1&taxonomyId=3233.

3. "Lakewood, Washington, Construction contractor, 19-CA-31580" (NLRP filed complaint for employees who were protected when appearing in YouTube video about hazardous work conditions) and "Hartford, Connecticut, Emergency medical response company, 34-CA-012576" (NLRB filed complaint of unlawful firing of employee who criticized supervisor on Facebook posting) Protected Concerted Activity, National Labor Relations Board.
   http://www.nlrb.gov/concerted-activity.

4. September 2012 Gallup poll reports that 52 percent of employees are not engaged and 18 percent are actively disengaged; http://www.gallup.com/poll/157397/half-don-strengths-throughout-day.aspx; http://www.gallup.com/poll/155924/mondays-not-blue-engaged-employees.aspx.

5. According to the National Institute of Mental Health, "An estimated 26.2 percent of Americans ages 18 and older—about one in four adults—suffer from a diagnosable mental disorder in a given year." See Kessler RC, Chiu WT, Demler O, Walters EE, "Prevalence, severity, and comorbidity of twelve-month DSM-IV disorders in the National Comorbidity Survey Replication (NCS-R)," *Archives of General Psychiatry* 62, no. 6, (June 2005): 617–27.

6. Mikal E. Belicove, "Social Media Users Are Squeakier Wheels When It Comes to Customer Service," Entrepreneur

.com on NBCNews.com; http://www.msnbc.msn.com/id/
47314679/ns/business-small_business/t/social-media-
users-are-squeakier-wheels-when-it-comes-customer-ser-
vice/.

Chapter 5 Toxics

1. A 2010 study reported in *Behavioral Sciences and the Law* found
   that 4 percent of a sample of corporate managers met a clinical
   threshold for being labeled psychopaths, compared with 1 percent for the population at large. See William Deresiewicz, "Capitalists and Other Psychopaths," *New York Times,* May 12, 2012,
   http://www.nytimes.com/2012/05/13/opinion/sunday/fables-
   of-wealth.html; P. Babiak, C. S. Neumann, and R. D. Hare, "Corporate psychopathy: Talking the walk," *Behavioral Sciences and
   the Law* 28, no. 2: 174–93.

Chapter 9 Go Ahead, Complain

1. See Robin M. Kowalski's article "Whining, Griping and Complaining: Positivity in the Negativity," *Journal of Clinical Psychology*
   58, no. 9, (Sept 2002): 1023–35.

References

Allen, Lorri and Linda Swindling, *Say It Right: Converse with Confidence, Tact & Care.* Reprint ed. Flower Mound, TX: Walk the Talk, 2010.

Babiak, Paul and Robert D. Hare, *Snakes in Suits: When Psychopaths Go to Work.* Reprint ed. New York: HarperCollins Publishers, 2006.

Belicove, E. Mikal, "Social Media Users Are Squeakier Wheels When It Comes to Customer Service," MSNBC.com, http://www.msnbc .msn.com/id/47314679/ns/business-small_business/t/social-media-users-are-squeakier-wheels-when-it-comes-customer-service/#.UJPyc44UX5Y.

Buffington, Sherry, *Who's Got the Compass? I Think I'm Lost! A Guide to Finding Your Ideal Self.* Second ed. Dallas, TX: QuinStar Publishing, 2013.

Carnegie, Dale, *How to Win Friends & Influence People.* Reissue ed. New York: Simon & Schuster, 2009.

Cloud, Henry and John Townsend, *Boundaries: When to Say YES, When to Say NO, to Take Control of Your Life.* Revised ed. Grand Rapids, Michigan: Zondervan, 1992.

Dawson, Roger, *Secrets of Power Negotiating, 15th Anniversary Edition: Inside Secrets from a Master Negotiator.* Pompton Plains, NJ: Career Press, 2010.

Deresiewicz, William, "Capitalists and Other Psychopaths," NYTimes.com, http://www.nytimes.com/2012/05/13/opinion/sunday/fables-of-wealth.html?_r=0.

Dolan, Patrick John, *Negotiate Like the Pros*. New York: LawTalk Publications, 2001.

Fisher, Roger and William Ury, *Getting to Yes: Negotiating Agreement without Giving In*. Revised ed. New York: Penguin Books, 2001.

Goleman, Daniel, *Emotional Intelligence: 10th Anniversary Edition; Why It Can Matter More Than IQ*. 10th Anniversary ed. New York: Bantam, 2006.

Gordon, Jon, *The Energy Bus: 10 Rules to Fuel Your Life, Work, and Team with Positive Energy*. Hoboken, NJ: John Wiley & Sons, 2007.

Gordon, Jon, *The No Complaining Rule: Positive Ways to Deal with Negativity at Work*. Hoboken, NJ: John Wiley & Sons, 2008.

Grote, Dick, *Discipline without Punishment: The Proven Strategy That Turns Problem Employees into Superior Performers,* 2nd ed. New York: AMACOM, 2006.

Harter, Jim, "Mondays Not So 'Blue' for Engaged Employees," Gallup.com, http://www.gallup.com/poll/155924/Mondays-Not-Blue-Engaged-Employees.aspx.

Kowalski, M. Robin, "Whining, Griping and Complaining: Positivity in the Negativity," *Journal of Clinical Psychology* 58, no. 9 (September 2002): 1023–1035.

Levinson, Meridith, "How to Fire People the Right Way," CIO.com, http://www.cio.com/article/692778/How_to_Fire_People_the_Right_Way.

Mackay, Harvey, *Swim with the Sharks without Being Eaten Alive: Outsell, Outmanage, Outmotivate, and Outnegotiate Your Competition (Collins Business Essentials)*. Reprint ed. New York: Ballantine Books, 2005.

Scott, Susan, *Fierce Conversations—Achieving Success at Work & In Life, One Conversation at a Time.* Reprint edition. New York: Berkley Trade, 2004.

Stone, Douglas, Bruce Patton, and Sheila Heel, *Difficult Conversations: How to Discuss What Matters Most.* Revised ed. New York: Penguin Books, 2010.

Swindling, Linda, *Get What You Want: Harness the Power of Positive Influence, Persuasion & Negotiation.* 6th reprint ed. Flower Mound, TX: Walk the Talk, 2010.

Whitehurst, Mel, *What Leaders Can Do to Diminish the Destructive Effects of Workplace Depression and Anxiety,* Plano, Texas: Kindle edition, Kindle e-Book, 2011.

Winget, Larry, *Shut Up, Stop Whining, and Get a Life: A Kick-Butt Approach to a Better Life,* 2nd ed. Hoboken, NJ: John Wiley & Sons, 2011.

Witters, Dan, Jim Asplund, and Jim Harter, "Half in U.S. Don't Use Their Strengths Throughout the Day," Gallup.com, http://www.gallup.com/poll/157397/half-don-strengths-throughout-day.aspx.

Acknowledgments

This book would not have been possible without Zan Jones and her invaluable insight, resources, and support. To the master of creativity and all things visual, Tim Cocklin, thank you for being patient, developing a rocking website, and creating the fun graphics found throughout.

Hugs and a huge thanks to Ginger Shelhimer, Elaine Morris, and Dave Lieber, whose counsel, advice, and creativity are limitless. Thank you to Dianna Booher and Howard Putnam, your expertise, support, mentoring, and friendship go beyond measure.

A big shout-out to the Wiley team, including Matt Holt, Adrianna Johnson, Susan Moran, and Christine Moore, and to Mike Freeland, whose cover inspired so many of the graphics in this book. Thank you to Lorri Allen, friend and coauthor of the *Passport to Succes, Say It Right: Converse with Confidence, Tact & Care*. Who knew that one page would prompt a conference discussion, a newsletter, and later a book? Thanks to Eric Harvey for his encouragement and for republishing the *Passports to Success* book series and welcoming me into his Walk the Talk family.

Thanks to an incredible expert panel of psychologists, psychiatrists, human resources professionals, communication specialists, and those who specialize in organizational behavior. Those who helped identify the individual Complainer traits for the surveys include Dr. Susan Battley, Dianna Booher, Joe Calloway, Chris Clarke-Epstein, Tim Durkin, Roxanne Emmerich, Dr. Susan Fletcher, Zan Jones, Gina Morgan, Elaine Morris, Dr. Terry Paulson, Mark Sanborn, Stu Schlackman, Joe Sherren, Nancy Starr, Brandon Walker, and Joyce Wood, with special appreciation to Drs. Sherry Buffington and Mel Whitehurst for your time and expert advice on how people communicate, interact, and think. Any errors are entirely mine.

In addition to those mentioned above, several gave their time and efforts to review scenarios and strategy, send surveys to peers, and provide valuable advice. Thanks go to Jason Aurora, Elaine Biech, Anne Bruce, Kip Eads, Betty Garrett, Amanda Gore, Dick Grote, Kris Harrison, Cindy Hartner, Dave Hill, Marc Hrisko, Chris James, Neen James, Christy Libby, Al Lucia, Michele Lucia, Bill Lynch, Teri Sjodin, Brenda Villareal, and Ken Wright. Special thanks to Suzanne Livingston for introducing the concept of *contribution*, to Sheryl Roush for *brilliance* in editing suggestions, *and* to Melinda Marcus, who sees opportunities where no one thinks to look.

Thank you to the more than 1,000 people who completed the survey and shared their work drama experiences and solutions. You'll see your contributions throughout. Thank you to Constant Contact for great support on our monthly *Success eTips* and Complainer survey. Thank you to all who sent research and appeared in videos *including* Valerie Cade, Christine Cashen, Dale Irvin, Willie Jolly, Jeanne Robertson, Steve Spangler, and Jana Stanfield. Kudos to all who forwarded this survey to their circles of friends. And props to Phill Martin and Hariett Meyerson who know how to *get the word out*.

Special thanks to those who went beyond the call of duty, including Julie Alexander, Sherry Andrus, Chris Arrendondo, David Avrin, Andrea Bahr, Audrey Baker, Donna Bender, Janita Byars, Amber Canceres, Eric Chester, Marsha Clark, Brian Collette, Peggy Collins, Sherry DeLaGarza, Charmaine Drinnon, Robert Ferguson, Candace Fitzpatrick, Marti Fox, Scott Friedman, Sue Fry, Joey Funke, Susan Gatton, Penny Glasscock, Adele Good, Robert Hartner, David Hira, Michael Hoffman, Chad Hymas, Rexanne Ingram, Tom Ingram, Leena John, Ron Kerr, Jeff Klein, Joyce Knudsen, Rick Kolster, Nancy McGraw, Kelley Moore, Sue Ogle, Suzie Oliver, Anna Parkins, Bryan Pasquale, Sally Roos Pasquale, Holly Peck, Doug Petersen, Chris Price, Phil Resch, Dana Rhoden, Russ Riddle, Gary Rifkin, Ed Robinson, Tom Sheives, Laura Stack, Marilyn Stewart, Mark Thompson, Liz Wilson, Monica Wofford, Lisa Zahn, and Cindy Zebroski, *and* to Vince Poscente, who thinks the book's title should be *Put a Cork in It*.

Thank you to my friends and colleagues at the National Speakers Association and NSA/North Texas, who years ago assured me that writing books and speaking for a living was possible. Thank you to my clients, especially Ericsson, HSMAI, Irving CVB, Dallas CVB, IAEE, ISES, MPI, NAWIC, PCMA, PPAI, TxACOM, SHRM, WBC/Southwest, and Professionals in Retail Service Management, who called attention to the Complainer and Energy Drain topic and helped develop solutions that work. Thanks to the Vistage community and to the Breakthroughs in Action tribe for showing me breakthroughs are possible for people and their organizations. Thanks to Judy Beller, Jennifer Stuart, Kimberly Wadsworth, and Jimi Willis for managing to keep me sane and keep other work progressing as I wrote this book.

Finally, a special thank you to my family: Pat and Byron Byars, my mom and dad, are always my encouragers and editors. To my sister KarenAnne Hall, brother Trey Byars, to Zoe, Ian, and Laura, and to my sis- and bro-in-law Stacy and Tim Mackey, thank you for providing support and insight and for showing me how to survive tough situations and drama without whining. Parker and Taylor, you are great kids. You don't complain about all of the things you could, you contribute so much to this world, and you have changed my life for the better. *And* Gregg, you are my confidant, best friend, and biggest supporter. Marrying you was the smartest decision ever—no complaints!

About the Author

From the courtroom to the boardroom, Linda Byars Swindling, JD, CSP, knows firsthand about engaging in high-stakes communications, negotiating workplace drama, and influencing decision makers. Her specialty is helping people communicate powerfully so that others will listen.

Linda first addressed employment and workplace communication issues as a successful attorney and a mediator, which led her to working as a consultant and an executive coach. When her book *The Consultant's Legal Guide* (coauthored with Elaine Biech) was released in 2000, Linda left her legal practice to focus full-time on Journey On, her Dallas-based, woman-owned business that offers customized training, strategic consulting, and executive coaching. In addition, Linda delivers keynote speeches and workshops at corporate and association meetings, events, and conventions.

A Certified Speaking Professional, Linda is a contributing editor, author and the coauthor of several books, and the creator of the popular *Passports to Success* book series, which includes titles such as *Get What You Want, Say It Right, At Your Service,* and *Set the Standard.*

In addition to service on several local boards, Linda has served as a Vistage chair, a national officer of the National Speakers

Association and is a past-president of the National Speakers Association/North Texas. Linda has worked with boards of directors, organizational teams, CEOs, key decision makers, and high potentials. A graduate of Texas Tech University and School of Law, her clients include the Fortune 500, companies from a wide variety of industries, governmental bodies, and many international associations. Despite a few remarks to her husband of 25 years and their two teenagers, she has not been a Complainer while writing this book. *Perhaps* a complaint or two did cross her mind but she stopped them. *Promise.*

About the Author